The Miracle of Gratitude

by

Toyosi Onwuemene

OPG

Onwuemene Publishing Group

Dedication

For Daddy Onwuemene, who showed me that the real miracle of

gratitude is inward transformation.

Table of Contents

Foreword

The Sin of Ingratitude

"If you take God for granted, you will be grounded."

"Because that, when they knew God, they glorified him not as God, neither were thankful; but became vain in their imaginations, and their foolish heart was darkened" (Romans 1:21).

"When thou hast eaten and art full, then thou shalt bless the LORD thy God for the good land which he hath given thee" (Deut. 8:10).

*This know also, that in the last days perilous times shall come. For men shall be lovers of their own selves, covetous, boasters, proud, blasphemers, disobedient to parents, **unthankful**, unholy, (2 Tim. 3:1-2).*

Ingratitude has become a great affliction that has affected our generation. We take so many things for granted; our health, family, job, and even the oxygen we breathe in daily.

Someone said: "I was weeping for lack of shoe until I met someone with lack of feet." No matter how bad you think it is for you, your case is still better than someone else.... So, give thanks.

Ingratitude is our failure to acknowledge and show appreciation for good things we have received from God. It is one of the traits of this end time. Thanksgiving is one important sacrifice a believer must render to God from time to time. Jesus Himself demonstrated thankfulness to God. Giving of thanks opens the door to many miracles and ingratitude does the opposite.

A grateful mind is a great mind; the person who has stopped being thankful has fallen asleep in life. The children of Israel, while going through their wilderness experience, never quite understood the place of thanking God for the benefits He showered on them. They never thanked Him for the manna, so their meal did not change for forty years. Some of us have bitterness against God, a grudge for something He has not done. Let praise release this bitterness.

Toyosi has done a great justice to this topic "The Miracle of Gratitude." I hope that, as you read and meditate on the pages of this book, you will go from "Thanksgiving" to "Thanksliving."

Give thanks!

Pastor (Dr.) Bisi Tofade

Introduction

¹⁸"The Spirit of the Lord is upon Me, Because He has anointed Me To preach the gospel to the poor; He has sent Me to heal the brokenhearted, To proclaim liberty to the captives And recovery of sight to the blind, To set at liberty those who are oppressed; ¹⁹To proclaim the acceptable year of the Lord." Luke 4:17-19

I didn't set out to write this book. It was gifted to me through an unlikely series of events that unfolded during the United States Thanksgiving holiday of 2022. The story began with a phone call from Pastor Bisi.

Pastor Bisi is my Pastor of about 20 years and the Senior Pastor of Jubilee Christian Church International Chapel of Victory. He called me on a Sunday afternoon following our annual Mountain Movers Conference. Because the conference marked our end-of-the-year fast, it was a season in which I was more open than usual to the Lord's voice. In that season, His voice came through to me more readily and I was open to new revelation.

Nevertheless, when Pastor Bisi called me that Sunday afternoon, I didn't think his phone call unusual. I guessed he was calling because someone in the church had a medical need that I, as a physician, could help meet. But I was wrong. The call had nothing

INTRODUCTION

to do with medicine. Instead, Pastor Bisi asked, " Will you share the message next Sunday?"

I was stunned. Me, share the message? No way! I wasn't prepared to share the message. Preaching to the congregation was not on my to-do list (ever). Surely, I thought, Pastor Bisi should have asked someone who was qualified. I was not an ordained minister. I had no titled position in the church. In fact, at the time, I was in a season of an extended break from serving in church ministry. For goodness sakes, I was a church benchwarmer! For these reasons, I was embarrassed by and felt unworthy to receive Pastor Bisi's request. But instead of verbalizing my objections, I mouthed a dutiful "Yes, of course," while the reel of objections played silently in my mind, impairing my ability to hear.

As Pastor Bisi shared sermon details, including the title of the message, I couldn't hear him. I was distracted. I kept thinking, "There is no way this is happening. No. I can't be the one to share the message. Not me. Not now."

It was no surprise then that I got off the phone and promptly forgot everything Pastor Bisi said, including the title of the message. During our conversation, I had deliberately spoken the title out loud three times so I wouldn't forget it. But now, for the life of me, I couldn't remember what it was. So, I turned to my husband, Chiedu, and asked him, "What was the title of the message again?" Chiedu said, "I don't know. Pastor wasn't talking to me; he was talking to you!" Chiedu had a good point; but it didn't help me. I was still stuck. What was that title again? Chiedu, always practical, recommended that I call Pastor Bisi back. What! Call Pastor Bisi and admit that I had not been listening to the most important piece of the conversation? No way!

So, instead of taking the simple step and making the call, I spent the next few hours racking my brains, trying to jog my memory for the title. Was it "The Miracle of Thanksgiving," "The Importance of Thanksgiving," or "The Miracle of Gratitude?" None of these titles clicked. I had not one clue. As the hours passed, I realized that no matter how hard I tried, I would not recall the title on my own. If I didn't ask Pastor Bisi now, I risked preaching the wrong message and embarrassing myself later. So, I summoned up courage and sent a text message. Pastor Bisi's return text confirmed the title as "The Miracle of Gratitude."

Having cleared the title hurdle, I turned next to the problem of what to say. Surely Pastor could have asked me to preach a more exciting message. Gratitude? Really? Gratitude was . . . so . . . predictably . . . Thanksgiving! Was there really anything new to share about gratitude? Surely by now, every Thanksgiving message had done gratitude justice. What could I share about gratitude that would be new?

But even as these thoughts raged, ideas began forming in my mind about different ways in which I could shed new light on an ancient concept. I recognized in that moment that it was the Holy Spirit dropping ideas in my mind and became relieved. I did have something to share after all. Now, instead of trepidation, came a growing excitement about the message.

But even as my excitement grew, I was still stuck feeling unqualified. I was an academic physician and not a preacher. I had credibility when I talked about matters of health but not matters of faith. Plus, it had been so long since I served in church ministry that many members of the congregation would not recognize me. People would wonder who I was. They would ask where I came from. They would wonder why I was the one preaching instead of their trusted and beloved pastor. I wasn't even an acceptable substitute. I was no big-name preacher; I was a no-name preacher. Surely, no one would want to hear from me. There was no way I was the right person to deliver the message. How could the Lord have chosen me?

As I pondered these questions before the Lord, He gently encouraged me with a story from Scripture called the Parable of the Sower (Matthew 13:3-8). In this story, a sower (farmer) went out to sow seed. Some seed fell by the wayside, some on stony ground, others among thorns, and others on good ground. The seed that fell on good ground yielded a crop that was sometimes 30-, 60-, or 100-fold.

THE MIRACLE OF GRATITUDE

From this story, I recognized that the sower could not have been a professional. A professional sower would have understood that seed costs money. Seed is precious. You don't take precious seed and just throw it anywhere. Precious seed is intentionally planted. First the ground is prepared, and the seed carefully planted. Next, the seed is watered, weeds removed, pests destroyed, and its progress carefully watched until it matures to become a harvest. This process was different from that used by the "unprofessional" sower in this story who went about throwing seed, not knowing exactly where the seed would fall. That the seed produced any harvest at all was the real miracle.

In the Parable of the Sower, the miracle of the seed was in its power to grow. The seed had the power to grow anywhere that it landed. When it landed by the wayside, the seed was taken by the birds before it had a chance to grow. However, when it landed on stony ground, the seed grew quickly but could not produce a harvest because there was no depth of earth to sustain it. When the seed landed among thorns, it grew; but it couldn't produce a harvest because the thorns choked it. It was not until the seed landed on good ground that it had the sustained growth that produced an incredible harvest. Therefore, the harvest did not depend on the skill of the sower, but on the power of the **_seed_** (the Word) to grow anywhere it landed. The harvest also depended on the preparedness of the **_ground_** (the people).

INTRODUCTION

Every time the word lands on good ground, it produces a harvest. This power of the Word is demonstrated by the story of the prophet Jonah (Jonah 1-4). Jonah reluctantly preached a message to the people of Nineveh that could be summarized as follows: "Forty days and y'all gonna die!" (Jonah 3:4). This message may have been the shortest (and worst) delivery in all Scripture.

So, given the message's brevity and the "awfulness" of its delivery, it was a surprise, even to Jonah, that it brought the entire city to repentance. The message traveled, indirectly, to Nineveh's king, who heard it and repented. He called for a fast that was proclaimed to the entire nation. And all Nineveh's people, even its animals, fasted and cried out to the Lord in repentance.

So, even though Jonah's message was delivered reluctantly and poorly, like the sower's seed, it brought about a miraculous harvest of transformation. Therefore, the transformation came, not from the speaker, but from the Word, which has power to produce a harvest every time it lands on good ground.

Good ground is ground that has been prepared to receive the Word before it arrives. In good ground, the soil has been prepared, stones removed, and thorns dealt with in advance of the word. And after the Word comes, additional work is needed to water the ground, remove the weeds, and destroy pests. When done consistently, this work produces a harvest that is 30-, 60-, or 100-fold greater than what was originally sown. Therefore, good ground is always prepared to produce a harvest whenever it encounters the word.

With the Lord's encouragement, I had a renewed sense of peace about the message. Like the "unprofessional" sower, I would deliver the message without worrying about the outcome. Like Jonah, I would preach the message and trust the Holy Spirit to minister it to each hearer in the place where they needed it most. I did not need to be eloquent, graceful, or funny. I needed only to share the Word as I understood it. Then I could trust the Lord to use His Word to impact His people. This revelation was similar to the one Paul the Apostle shared in the following Scripture:

> *And my speech and my preaching were not with persuasive words of human wisdom, but in demonstration of the Spirit and of power, that your faith should not be in the wisdom of men but in the power of God* (1 Corinthians 2:4-5; *New King James Version*).

Having now fully accepted my commission to preach the message, I headed out of town to celebrate Thanksgiving with my family. That year, we celebrated Thanksgiving in a large farmhouse in Adams, Tennessee, with sixteen members of our extended family. Surrounded by family and celebration in the vast expanse of farmland, I was immersed in the perfect atmosphere to receive God's word regarding gratitude. And as the week progressed, bits and pieces of the sermon came to me, and I typed these words into my computer or dictated them into my phone until I had the entire

INTRODUCTION

sermon script. I rehearsed the script several times until it was embedded in my spirit. Then Sunday morning rolled around, and I trusted that the Holy Spirit would help me deliver the message.

On Sunday morning, the message I shared came out differently from what I had imagined (you can watch or listen to it on YouTube: https://youtu.be/VQjOwkvj1VI?t=2568). I had underestimated the time to transition from praise and worship; so, I ended up with less time for the message than I planned. For this reason, I did not read as many scriptures or share all the stories I had planned.

After the message, I kept feeling as if I had left out important parts. For weeks following the message, new scriptures would come into my mind that I wish I had shared. I began to wonder why I had invested as much time as I had writing out stories and scriptures that now would never be shared. How could words so inspired be forever confined to my computer without being shared with others in a meaningful way?

As I reflected on these thoughts, the seed of an idea began to take shape: What if I took the sermon script, combined it with the live sermon audio, and wrote a book for all to read? In doing that, the Lord's people would have the unabridged version of the message with details added for clarity. And so began the writing process.

First I used my detailed sermon script to create a draft. Then I updated the draft using the live sermon audio transcript. As I edited, wrote, and rewrote the pages, the ideas felt more compelling and the words timely. The more I meditated on the content, the more ideas filled my mind, many of which came to me during my morning prayer walks. Slowly but surely, over many iterations, the multidimensional nature of gratitude and its accompanying miracles came together to form this book.

The final piece of the book's puzzle came together for me about two weeks after the message when I finally summoned up the courage to ask Pastor Bisi, "Why?" "Why (of all people in the church) did you ask me to preach this message?" Pastor Bisi said, "I prayed about it, and the Lord told me." This simple statement, which is so characteristic of Pastor Bisi, caused me to pause and reflect until I came to this understanding: There was a seed of the message inside me; but it didn't come alive until I was asked to preach the message. And in the process of creating a message to share with my church family, I was creating the foundation of a book that I would eventually share with you. I was invited to preach a message so that this book could be written for you.

As you read this book, which has your name on it (in the spirit), may it transform your life to become one that is filled with gratitude in multiple dimensions. And may you grow into the place of gratitude-filled relationship with the Lord Jesus, the One who makes all gratitude possible. Shalom!

Gratitude and Miracles

You did not choose Me, but I chose you and appointed you that you should go and bear fruit, and that your fruit should remain, that whatever you ask the Father in My name He may give you (John 15:6).

He chose me

My life is an unfolding story of God's principle of election. I was born in a small town (Ileṣa) in a state unknown to the general international community (Oṣun) in a country considered to be "third world" (Nigeria) to parents for whom English was a second language (Yẹmi and Anikẹ). So, then, how did I get here? How did I come to be living in one of the wealthiest nations of the world (the United States), as a physician at a major academic institution (Duke University), preaching a message at an internationally recognized church (Jubilee), and writing a book about gratitude and miracles? Who am I and how I did I come to be here at this time and in this season?

If a "logical" person had been asked to make predictions about the course of my life based on my birthplace, gender, and skin color, they would have predicted a different course for my life. If their prediction did not include early death from infant mortality, perhaps it would have included death in early childhood from infectious disease. But if their predictions allowed me to survive to adulthood, perhaps they would have predicted that I wouldn't have learned to speak English and that, if I even went to school, I was likely to have dropped out without a diploma. And if I was lucky enough to graduate high school, at most, I would be living within the radius of my birthplace and there would certainly be no international travel involved. The math doesn't add up. I shouldn't be here. But I am. I am here because the Lord chose me.

I recognize that the Lord chose me because every consequential thing that has occurred in my life has been out of my control. The Lord chose me to be born to parents who worked and put themselves through school, to a father who made a living as a diplomat, and to a family that traveled internationally. He chose my father to be posted to Jamaica at a time when I would be applying to college. He chose me to receive a scholarship I didn't apply for to go to a private college whose application deadline I intentionally missed because I didn't want to go there. He chose me to go to a medical school that was not my first choice, to attend my backup residency program after my first choice rejected me, and to start an academic position in a role I did not want. He chose me to be married to a man I initially chased away and gave me children I did not select. Most importantly, He chose me to receive His gift of salvation so I could walk in relationship with Him, hear His voice, and bring His message to His people.

GRATITUDE AND MIRACLES

I am one of "the chosen." I am in the company of people throughout biblical history whose lives were marked by choices outside their control. This company includes Abraham, who was chosen to go on a journey with no clear destination (Genesis 12); Moses, who came across a "talking bush" that sent him on an impossible mission (Exodus 3); Deborah, who didn't train for the battle she helped win (Judges 4); Rahab, whose unlikely customers turned out to be spies (Joshua 2); David, a king who was not invited to his own coronation ceremony (1 Samuel 16); Esther, a reluctant competitor in a chauvinistic beauty pageant (Esther 2)**;** and Paul, who was blinded while on a road trip with a sinister mission (Acts 9). Like me, these people were chosen by the Lord to be born in a specific era, to "discover" Him, and then to live and work to fulfill the mission to which He called them (Acts 17:26). These people, and others like them who came before me, are the great cloud of witnesses that encourage and cheer me on (Hebrews 12:1).

Reflecting on the improbability of my life's course and the incredible company to which I belong, I am grateful for a life that both began as a miracle and continues to unfold as a miracle. I am grateful to the Lord for choosing me, for gifting me an incredible story, and for giving me grace and ability to share it. Yes, my heart is full of gratitude.

Thank you with a great attitude

THE MIRACLE OF GRATITUDE

Here in the United States, gratitude is often associated with the Thanksgiving holiday, that time once a year in November when we set aside a day to be thankful. For many people, the Thanksgiving holiday is an annual opportunity to remember all the good things that have happened in their lives. However, some people celebrate a period of Thanksgiving more than once a year. Some people set aside a monthly period, or perhaps, a weekly period of Thanksgiving. But even fewer people take time to celebrate thanksgiving and show gratitude as a daily routine.

Whatever our schedule of thanksgiving celebrations, showing gratitude tends to be associated with saying, "Thank you." In our family, at our Thanksgiving dinner table, we usually take turns to say what we are thankful for. We say, "Thank you" to each other and the Lord. But, even though the words, "Thank you" are an unmistakable expression of gratitude, gratitude is not just about saying "Thank you."

If gratitude is not just about saying, "thank you," then what is it? To find out, let's look its formal definition:

> *The quality or condition of being grateful; a warm sense of appreciation of kindness received, involving a feeling of goodwill towards the benefactor and a desire to do something in return.*[1]

---

[1] 'Gratitude, n.', *OED Online* (Oxford University Press) <https://www.oed.com/view/Entry/80957> [accessed 21 April 2023].

GRATITUDE AND MIRACLES

What I love about this definition is that it describes gratitude as a "quality or condition" of being grateful. Thus, gratitude points to our inner expression of thankfulness. When we show gratitude, we use words and actions to express feelings that may not be well captured by words alone. For this reason, gratitude is an expression of an inner feeling that (usually) comes out in the words, "thank you." However, because gratitude is a "quality of being thankful," gratitude cannot be expressed fully with words alone.

It is possible to say "thank you" without feeling any gratitude. You can try this thankless gratitude experiment with a partner or with yourself using a mirror. First, say, "Thank you" a few times with the worst attitude possible. Next, say, "Thank you" with a feeling of deep sincere gratitude. Did you feel the difference? The first "thank you" may have been accompanied by bad feelings and, probably, an ugly facial expression. The second "thank you" may have been accompanied by inner warmth and a smile.

The same words, "thank you," said with and without sincerity, produced a different experience in you, the speaker. Imagine then, the experience for the hearer. In the same way that we feel the difference between a sincere and insincere "thank you," our hearers also feel the difference. For this reason, gratitude is best expressed when thankful words match thankful feelings. True thankfulness is shown when our words match the attitude with which we express gratitude. Therefore, for the purposes of this book, I define gratitude as "thankfulness with great attitude!"

THE MIRACLE OF GRATITUDE

A gratitude-attitude mismatch is a problem for Spirit

When there is a mismatch between a person's thankful words and their unthankful attitude, we can tell the difference because we are spirits, and we live in a body. Our body (ears) may hear the words, "Thank you," but our spirit discerns the attitude with which the words are spoken. It feels weird when someone says "thank you" with a bad attitude because there is a mismatch between what our ears hear and what our spirit experiences.

The spirit's experience of gratitude is most pertinent to the Lord, who is Spirit (John 4:24). His experience of our gratitude is primarily defined by our attitude. The Lord is never distracted by our words. He goes straight to the attitude or the spirit with which we show gratitude. This principle is illustrated in in Isaiah 29:13, in which the Lord says:

> *"These people draw near with their mouths And honor Me with their lips, But have removed their hearts far from Me."*

So, while, sometimes, we can fool a person with an insincere thank you, we can never fool the Lord. Our inability to fool the Lord is relevant to the fruit that gratitude produces.

Miracles: The fruit of gratitude

The expression of our gratitude, or lack thereof, produces a seed that germinates. As we noted earlier, the attitude that accompanies our gratitude is heard louder by the spirit. Therefore, we can think of the attitude expressed by gratitude as our spirit expressing words. Words matter because they are the foundation of everything we see. Words spoken by the Spirit are the foundation of the visible world in which we live. This sentiment is expressed beautifully in Hebrews 11:3:

> *By faith we understand that the worlds were framed by the word of God, so that the things which are seen were not made of things which are visible.*

The words of God that framed the universe were not uttered by a physical being that can be seen; they were uttered by an invisible Spirit. It is this Spirit whose image we are created in.

> *Then God said, "Let Us make man in Our image, according to Our likeness; let them have dominion over the fish of the sea, over the birds of the air, and over the cattle, over all the earth and over every creeping thing that creeps on the earth."* (Genesis 1:26)

Therefore, just as the Spirit of God and His thoughts spoke inaudible words that framed the universe, our spirits speak inaudible words that frame our own personal universe. Every time we say "thank you" with a grateful attitude, our spirit speaks these words out loud so that they frame our world. When our spirit shows gratitude for something good, it says, "I like this thing and I want more of it." And so, our spirit begins to create a world that matches what we like. For this reason, we will always get more of what we appreciate.

In showing gratitude, our spirit sends a message to the universe that what we have seen is good, which makes room for the next phase of creation. In Genesis 1, after each new creation, the Lord took time to review it and declare that it was good, thereby showing gratitude. And having declared that His new creation was good, the Lord then went on to create "more good."

The last thing that God created was people, following which He declared that His creation was "very good" (Genesis 1:31). And then He rested. The Lord was able to rest because His last "very good" creation was made in His image and likeness and, therefore, has His creative power. This same creative power is wielded by our spirits. Therefore, each time our creative spirit looks at the Lord's creation and declares, in gratitude, that it is good, it releases us to partner with the Lord and create the next thing. For this reason, gratitude, which our spirits express out loud to the universe, exists in different dimensions.

Dimensions of gratitude

Gratitude is multidimensional, which means that it has different aspects to it. In this book, I talk about gratitude in three dimensions. Think about these three dimensions in the same way as you would a three-dimensional shape. Each dimension by itself shows you a limited aspect of the shape. Thus, we define shapes according to their length, breadth, and depth. When all three dimensions are combined, a fuller, more complete, picture of the shape is revealed. As with shapes, different aspects of gratitude can be defined in three dimensions. All three dimensions combined give you the fullest picture of gratitude.

The dimension of gratitude we express depends on our underlying beliefs and experiences. These dimensions correspond to different expressive "words" spoken out loud by our spirits. When we express gratitude reluctantly, or not at all, it represents an underlying belief that not much has been done for us. Therefore, it is as if our spirit is saying out loud: "I don't have much to be thankful for." These "spirit words" go on to create a personal universe of "Not much to be thankful for." But, when we express gratitude enthusiastically, it represents an underlying belief that much has been done for us. It is as if our spirit is saying out loud: "I have so much to be thankful for." These "spirit words" go on to create a personal universe of "so much to be thankful for." Therefore, our beliefs and experiences about how much good there is or is not in our lives influence what our spirit communicates to create the universe we experience.

Our experiences of our environment can influence the type of gratitude we express. We express minimal or no gratitude (first dimension) when we perceive our environment to be limited or have scarce resources. Thus, "our spirit words" create more limited or scarce resources. We express enthusiastic gratitude (second dimension) when we perceive our environment to be abundant and filled with many good things. Thus, our "spirit words" create more abundance and fill our environment with more good things. But when we ignore our environment and decide to express gratitude no matter what (third dimension), our "spirit words" also create things that are environment-independent.

When we express gratitude in a way that is environment-independent, we look beyond our circumstances to the One who creates the environment. Therefore, the "spirit words" spoken in this state of gratitude create a universe that is "other worldly." An environment-independent gratitude shapes a universe that flows from the perspective of the One who is limitless.

Thus, environment-limited, environment-abundant, and environment-independent gratitude summarize the three dimensions of gratitude that I will share with you in this book. They also help frame the miracles that accompany them.

A miracle is defined as follows:

> *A marvellous event not ascribable to human power or the operation of any natural force and therefore attributed to supernatural, esp. divine, agency; esp. an act (e.g., of healing) demonstrating control over nature and serving as evidence that the agent is either divine or divinely favoured.*[2]

[2] 'Miracle, n.', *OED Online* (Oxford University Press) <https://www.oed.com/view/Entry/119052> [accessed 21 April 2023].

GRATITUDE AND MIRACLES

Each dimension of gratitude is associated with different kinds of miracles. First dimension of gratitude is an environment-dependent gratitude that experiences scarcity; therefore, miracles produced by first dimension gratitude are environment-bound and scarce. Second dimension gratitude is also an environment-dependent gratitude; but it experiences abundance. Therefore, the miracles produced by second dimension gratitude are environment-bound and abundant. Third dimension gratitude is an environment-independent gratitude that looks to the Lord as the limitless One who can create new environments. Therefore, the miracles produced by third dimension gratitude defy people's expectations and break the rules of the environment. We will cover each dimension of gratitude and its accompanying miracles in more detail in subsequent chapters.

The invitation

As we journey through this book together, I invite you to walk in the fullness of the miracle of gratitude by activating each dimension of gratitude. Although each dimension can stand alone and be understood in its individual detail, all three are needed to experience a full and miracle-filled life. Living a life of gratitude in only one dimension is possible; however, one-dimensional living is limited. For the miracle of gratitude to be experienced in its entirety, each dimension must be layered upon the other. Therefore, I invite you to follow me through the upcoming chapters as I explain each dimension in detail and show you how they are relevant to walking in the miraculous.

First, I will discuss *first dimension gratitude*, which unleashes a few miracles that are consistent with the human experience. Next, I will discuss *second dimension gratitude*, which unleashes exponential miracles in the specific area for which the gratitude is expressed. Then I will discuss *third dimension gratitude*, which creates miracles that defy human expectation. Finally, as a bonus, I will share a (not so secret) secret *fourth dimension*, which is the secret sauce that gives the first three dimensions synergy.

However, before we start our discussion of the three dimensions of gratitude, I must first warn you about a dimension of gratitude that you never want to be at. This dimension is the sub-zero dimension.

The Sub-Zero Dimension

Do all things without complaining and disputing (Philippians 2:14)

They did not want a crying baby

In 2014, I traveled with my husband and children to a wedding in San Francisco. When we arrived at the San Francisco airport, we took the shuttle to the building that housed the car rental companies. We arrived and found that the place was packed. It seemed that everybody and their brother had arrived at the exact same time. There must have been a major event that weekend because the lines were so long, they were unbelievable. With the number of people waiting in line, our estimated wait time was easily three hours or more. Resigned to our long wait, my husband, Chiedu, got in line, and I settled down with the children for the long wait.

A few minutes into our wait, our daughter, who was five months old at the time, started crying. The crying was not immediately a problem for me because, by this time, I had over two years of parenting experience under my belt, and I knew exactly what to do. I would get her cooing in no time. But I was wrong. She didn't stop crying. Whatever I did, it didn't work. I changed her diaper, tried to feed her, and rocked her back and forth; but it was useless.

THE MIRACLE OF GRATITUDE

No matter what I did, she just kept crying, and she was getting louder by the minute.

By now, I was getting frantic. People were giving me those looks — you know the kind you get (or give) when a mother just can't "control" her child. Although I could feel the angry looks directed at me, I worked hard to ignore them as I focused on soothing this child. But the long wait times had put people on edge. People were getting testy. No one was in the mood to tolerate a crying baby. I kept trying to calm her down; but she became more frustrated, and the crying intensified.

About twenty minutes into this drama, a lady from the rental company walked up to us. She could see that I was not making any meaningful progress with my crying baby. She kindly asked me if I had anybody in line waiting for a rental car. I pointed out Chiedu who, still in the far back of the line, was no closer to getting the rental than he had been when he first got in it. The lady picked him out and walked up to him. Then, she pulled Chiedu from his position and walked him to the front of the line. The front desk staff member promptly got his information and gave him the rental keys. And just like that, we were ready to leave.

Although we were relieved to have our rental sooner than we thought possible, it was clear that their "gift" was a practical gesture get rid of us and our crying baby. Through our crying baby, we had unleashed the effects of the sub-zero dimension.

THE SUB-ZERO DIMENSION

The sub-zero dimension produces miracles of multiplication by zero

The sub-zero dimension is a dimension where nobody should be. While I don't want to dignify it by giving it space in this book, I need to address this sub-zero dimension so you can recognize it and stay as far away from it as possible. I address the sub-zero dimension first because it is dangerous to your physical, mental, and spiritual health. The sub-zero dimension can literally kill you. If, by any chance, you happen to already be at this sub-zero dimension, I want to help you escape. To understand the dangers of living in the sub-zero dimension of gratitude, we're going to need to do a little bit of math. I promise it will not be anything too complicated. I assure you that sub-zero dimension math is math you can handle.

What do you get when you multiply any number by 0? You are correct. A number multiplied by 0 will always give you 0. Ok, let's do a few math problems. What is 1×0? How about 2×0? Ok 72×0? Ok, let's make it extra hard. What is 54 quintillion $\times 0$? Wow, you are good at this math. Any number, no matter how big, when multiplied by 0 will always give you 0.

Unfortunately, the math of the sub-zero dimension is actually worse than multiplying by 0 because sub-zero actually means "below zero." The math in the sub-zero dimension is actually multiplying by negative numbers. Living in the sub-zero dimension of gratitude will always leave you at or below zero. For this reason, you want to avoid the sub-zero dimension because, not only does it reduce you to zero or place you in a negative zone; but it will also reduce everyone around you to zero or below. The sub-zero dimension is the anti-gratitude dimension of **complaining**.

Complaining feels like a baby crying non-stop

Complaining is the sub-zero, anti-gratitude dimension where no miracles are produced. In fact, as we will soon discover, complaining may actually reverse miracles that have previously existed. Complaining is so awful that it is like a loud whining sound that no one can tolerate for long. After only a few minutes of hearing complaints, people are ready to do anything just to get it to stop. Therefore, complaining can be likened to the non-stop whining of a crying baby.

The Lord specially designed crying to seep into our psyche and upset us until we can't stand it. Crying bothers us so much that we will go to great lengths to make it stop. Many mothers can hear their baby's cry in their sleep and wake up to stop it. While many fathers may not have the equivalent gift, they certainly can't stand to hear their babies cry when they are awake during the day. The cry of a baby is so distressing that people will go to great lengths to fix whatever is wrong. It was the distress signal activated by our crying baby that led our car rental company to act quickly.

THE SUB-ZERO DIMENSION

When our daughter started crying, the people around us tolerated her crying until they reached breaking point. Tempers were flaring and people were losing patience. If someone didn't do something about it, something was about to explode. The crying bothered them so much, they needed to get it to stop. For the car rental company, the only way they knew how to fix their "problem" was to give us what we were looking for so that we would leave. They broke protocols of who gets to be served first so that we would remove the source of their distress.

When the lady pulled Chiedu out of the line to take him to the front desk, he did not suddenly acquire VIP status. He had not accumulated enough elite miles for special favors. He received "special favors" because the car rental company was trying to save themselves and their other customers from distress. They were "kind" because they wanted to be rid of us. On that day when there were more customers than they had capacity to accommodate, our crying baby was bad for morale. Neither the company staff or its customers could handle more crying so they did what they could to get rid of us and our crying baby.

What is interesting is that none of the other customers complained about our special treatment because it benefitted them too. No, they did not complain that Chiedu was cutting in line. No, they were not upset that the rental company was being unfair. No, they did not kick and scream that the rental company was giving Chiedu special favors and not them. Instead, everybody –

customers and staff alike – likely heaved a sigh of relief that we were gone. They were happy to be rid of us and our crying baby.

Although we could have naively interpreted our experience as having received a great gift, the "gift" was likely accompanied by a cursing heart (the spirit speaking bad words out loud). So, while their actions spoke one thing – understanding and kindness – the inner expression of their spirit was "We can't stand this. Get them out of here!" And so, the "miracle" they created was to remove us from their physical environment.

Like the crying of a baby in distress is the sound of complaining. The cry of complaining feels awful to the Lord. He hates complaining so much that He will go to great lengths to silence it. We see an example of the Lord's hatred of complaining in Numbers 14: 26-29. However, before we read this scripture, I want to give you some background.

They complained and the Lord got mad.

In Numbers 13, the Lord asked Moses to send out twelve men to spy out the land of Canaan. See, the people of Israel were formerly enslaved in Egypt and the Lord had delivered them with a mighty and outstretched hand (Exodus 14). Now, in fulfillment of His promise to their ancestor, Abraham (Genesis 15:18), He was ready to give them their own land. So, He asked Moses to choose twelve men – one man each from the twelve tribes of Israel – for a mission to spy out the land. The men went out as commanded and came back after forty days.

When they returned, the spy party expressed two different perspectives. The minority perspective, presented by Joshua and Caleb, was positive. They had a good report of the land. Their perspective was, "Wow! Our God is incredible and the land He has given us is good. Let's quickly go up and take over the land. With the Lord on our side, we're definitely going to make it" (*my paraphrase*). However, the majority perspective, presented by the other ten spies, was negative. They collectively said, "Sure the land is good; but the people in it are giants. The land devours its inhabitants; and there is no way we or our children can survive in it" (*my paraphrase*). They felt it was time to give up all they had gained and go back into slavery.

Their bad report quickly spread through the land. Before the day was over, the entire congregation was complaining. People started crying. They wished themselves dead. They even started discussing plans to select a new leader who would take them back to slavery in Egypt (Numbers 14:1-3). Through their negative report, the ten spies had unleashed a "plague" of complaining.

See, complaining is a contagious and deadly disease. Ten men complained and, in a matter of hours, the entire congregation was infected. By the time the infection spread to the people, it had worsened, leading people to cry in despair and change their life outlook. Not only did their outlook on the past change (they decided the Lord was out to destroy them); but they also began to imagine (or use their "spirit words" to create) a tragic future of disaster and destruction for both them and their children. The contagion started with only ten men; but it ultimately spread to the entire congregation.

And how many people were in the congregation? While the scriptures do not tell us explicitly, I guess that the congregation numbered at least a million people. In Numbers 11:21, Moses tells us that there were about 600,000 men. From the number of men, I estimate that there were at least as many, if not more, women and children. So, a conservative estimate is about 1.2 million people. Ten people started complaining and, within a matter of hours, at least 1.2 million people were infected.

Friend, that infection rate may be worse than any virus known to man. Imagine a virus spreading from ten people to over a million people in just a matter of hours. Infections don't spread that quickly but complaining does. The spread of complaining in our modern world is just as easy when you consider that one bad news report on one major network news channel can be transmitted to millions of people at once.[3] So, complaining spreads more easily than infections and may do more damage.

The spies who complained and the congregation infected by their complaining were ultimately reduced to zero, as we find out in the Lord's response in Numbers 14:26-29.

> [26] *And the Lord spoke to Moses and Aaron, saying,* [27] *"How long shall I bear with this evil congregation who complain against Me? I have heard the complaints which the children of Israel make against Me.* [28] *Say to them, 'As I live,' says the Lord, 'just as you have spoken in My hearing, so I will do to you:* [29] *The carcasses of you who have complained against Me shall fall in this wilderness, all of you who were numbered, according to your entire number, from twenty years old and above.*

So, the end result is that they lost their inheritance and eventually died in the wilderness . . . for complaining!

The Lord's reaction may seem drastic to you; but to understand it, we need to go back to what thoughts (spirit words) are created by the spirit of a complaining person. A complaining person declares out loud to the universe that their environment is horrible and no good can come out of it. These negative "spirit words" go to work to create the negative environment that is being declared until it

---

[3] Pew Research Center, 'Network News Fact Sheet', *Pew Research Center's Journalism Project* <https://www.pewresearch.org/journalism/fact-sheet/network-news/> [accessed 16 April 2023].

becomes the only reality of a complaining person. This situation describes the inverse of faith. It is negative faith or unbelief.

The power of negative faith or unbelief is demonstrated in Matthew 13:58:

> *Now He did not do many mighty works there because of their unbelief.*

The Lord Jesus was hindered from doing mighty works among His people because he was hindered by the power of unbelief, or negative faith in action. In the same way, imagine the combined power of over a million spirit voices of the spies and the congregation united in negative faith to keep God's promises from coming to pass. The Lord was up against a powerful force, and He moved quickly to break its power.

Negative faith or unbelief will continue to create a negative environment and hinder the Lord's move unless the cycle of negative "spirit words" being spoken to the universe is broken. Therefore, the Lord moved to remove the deadly creative force that was at work in the environment.

God dealt with the negative creative force in two phases. First, He sent a plague that killed the ten complaining spies immediately (Numbers 14:37). Then, over a period of about forty years, He allowed all the infected adult members of the congregation to die. Of the original adult congregation, the only two people who remained alive were Joshua and Caleb, who had partnered with the Lord to speak "spirit words" that created possibility.

Through their (positive) faith, Joshua and Caleb used "spirit words" to create a future that was consistent with the Lord's vision for His people: "We will win! The Lord will help us!! The Lord has given us the land!!!" And so, as the infected congregation speaking negative "spirit words" were dying, their positive "spirit words" remained to help a new generation create the life-giving environment that the Lord had wanted all along.

Venting is also complaining

By now, we have established that complaining is bad news; but what about venting? Isn't it OK to vent, even occasionally?

Consider the definition of complain:

> *To give expression to sorrow or suffering.*[4]

And contrast it with the definition of vent:

> *To relieve or unburden (one's heart or soul) in respect of feelings or emotions.*[5]

While both terms have different definitions, they seem awfully close to me.

---

[4] 'Complain, v.', *OED Online* (Oxford University Press) <https://www.oed.com/view/Entry/37612> [accessed 21 April 2023].
[5] 'Vent, v.2', *OED Online* (Oxford University Press) <https://www.oed.com/view/Entry/222211> [accessed 21 April 2023].

THE MIRACLE OF GRATITUDE

Sometimes, we feel as if we should get a free pass if our complaints are not directed against the Lord. We may simply be complaining about our environment or expressing our annoyance at someone who has done something to deserve it. Perhaps someone deserves our annoyance because they exercised poor judgment, made a wrong decision, or did something we consider bad. We may feel justified that we have a good reason for venting or complaining. However, all complaining, justified or unjustified, is displeasing to the Lord. Most of the time, the Lord hears our complaining as if we personally complained against Him.

In Numbers 17, we hear the Lord's personal take on inter-personal complaining. Prior to the events in this chapter, complaints about Aaron's leadership had been growing (Numbers 16). The leaders of the congregation felt that Aaron and Moses were not that special, but they were making themselves out to be better than everyone else (sound familiar?). Although these complaints were made directly against Aaron and Moses, the Lord took them personally. After all, it was the Lord who had chosen them as leaders, no matter how imperfect they were. Therefore, He devised a plan to stop their complaining.

Hear what the Lord says about this situation in Numbers 17:5.

> *"And it shall be that the rod of the man whom I choose will blossom; thus, I will rid Myself of the complaints of the children of Israel, which they make against you."*

THE SUB-ZERO DIMENSION

In this scripture, the Lord is essentially saying, "Aaron, I need to rid myself of the complaints they make against you because I take their complaining against you personally. I need to get rid of this problem, not for you; but for me."

No matter how cool our substitute words, complaining is still complaining. Whether it is "venting," "blowing off steam," or "stewing," these cool words are just synonyms for complaining. And all complaining is a horrible loud sound in the Lord's Spirit ears. The Lord hears the loud cry of a complaining spirit as a voice uttering "spirit words" of creative destruction that affects, not just the complainer, but also others around them. When our spirit's creative power is engaged in creating a negative environment that limits the Lord's move, He will sometimes go to great lengths to remove the complainer from the environment.

In the same way that the Lord dislikes complaining, we also hate to be complained about. We may not think twice about raising a complaint against someone else; but we certainly do not appreciate complaints that are brought against us. In general, people love to complain; but no one likes to be complained about.

Think back to the last time someone brought a complaint against or criticized you. How happy were you? How graciously did you respond? How easily did you give them what they wanted? If you answer these questions honestly, you may recognize that other people's complaints about you put you in a bad mood. But although we might hate it when other people complain about us, we don't mind as much when we are the ones doing the complaining. Before I knew better, I also loved to complain.

My husband would not complain

When Chiedu and I were first married, I was surprised to find that he did not like to complain. Even when I encouraged him to, he would not complain at all. No matter the circumstance, there was not one word of complaining: Zip, zilch, nada! Chiedu's lack of complaining was a problem for me because I was sure there was something wrong with him.

On a typical day of our early married years, I would come back from work and launch into a tirade about how one thing after another went wrong; and all hell broke loose; and everything was a disaster. And then I would tell him about what one person did wrong that led to another person's bad behavior, which led to things spiraling out of control. Then I would share about how everything came together to make a perfectly good day terrible. By the time I was done complaining, I had painted a vivid picture of an irredeemable, disastrous day at work, complete with histrionics.

Throughout my ranting, Chiedu would patiently listen and express his support; but he would not join me in complaining. Neither would he complain to me about his own day. No matter how much I prodded or tried to get him to complain about his job or his co-workers (and I could see plenty to complain about), he just wouldn't do it. By not complaining, Chiedu rained on my complaining parade. Clearly, Chiedu's problem was that he didn't understand the way complaining works.

How complaining works

In case you do not understand why Chiedu's lack of complaining was a problem for me, I want to help you understand how complaining works. Complaining "works" like a game of tennis in which there is a mutual volley of give and take. Therefore, complaining works best with a minimum of two people.

The first person starts by telling a terrible, "woe is me," or "the sky is falling" type story. While the first person is still in the middle of their personal tale of woe, the second person is not really listening. Instead, they are preparing their own response. While the first person is speaking, they are having a personal conversation in their heads about how they can top the first person with a bigger and better "tale of woe." And, since they are not really listening to the speaker, it doesn't take long to come up with something good. Therefore, as soon as there is a break in the first person's speech, the second person quickly interrupts.

As the second person shares their own story, you know they have done a good job when you see that their story has been carefully constructed to make the first look weak. "You think what happened to you was bad? Wait until you hear what happened to me." The second person now spins their own tale of woe while the first person "listens." But as it was when the roles were reversed, the listener is not listening but rather forming a counter story that makes their complaint more awful.

There is no natural end to this "game." Hardly does either party feel sufficiently satisfied that their own tale of woe was the worst. Therefore, this cycle repeats until both parties are either worn out or the conversation is cut short. By the time the conversation is over, both parties have spun tales of woe and disaster; but you wouldn't guess it from their smug expressions of satisfaction. What is happening internally is that each person is high-fiving themselves, thinking, "Yeah, she thought she had it bad and I showed her! I showed her whose problem was worse." So, each party is pleased with themselves; but the Lord, who is watching an evil creative force at work, is displeased.

At this time in my life, I didn't appreciate how much the Lord hated complaining (hey everyone was doing it!), so it was fortunate for me that Chiedu was no good at this game. I would complain and Chiedu would give nothing back. No, Chiedu would not play. And, because, the complaining game only works well with two or more willing parties, I could not up the ante, and my complaining sessions fizzled out. But it wasn't until about a decade later that I realized that I had been wrong to try to infect Chiedu with my complaining. As I began to understand the Lord's perspective about complaining, I saw how the Lord had been merciful to me.

THE SUB-ZERO DIMENSION

What I did not understand was that, to complain, directly or indirectly, is to deny the Lord's creative power. See, He is the One who hovered over the face of the earth in Genesis chapter 1 when it was formless and empty and there was darkness everywhere. It was His word that brought the world we see today out of the realm of the invisible (Hebrews 11:3). He is the same Lord who sits above the circle of the earth such that, compared to Him, its "inhabitants are like grasshoppers" (Isaiah 40:22). He is the One who "stretches out the heavens like a curtain and spreads them out like a tent to dwell in." He is the same Lord who is working everything together for our good because we love Him and are "called according to His purpose" (Romans 8:28).

He is the One who takes our mistakes and turns them into treasure, like He did for Abraham when he lied about his wife being his sister (Genesis 20:13) and David when he sinned with Bathsheba (2 Samuel 12). So, there is no circumstance, good or bad, that the Lord cannot recreate and turn around to become a blessing. For this reason, when I chose to complain instead of trust, I was telling Him that His arm is too short to save me, or His ear too deaf to hear me (Isaiah 59:1). When I chose to complain, I allowed my "spirit words" to work destructively instead of creatively. When I chose to complain, I worked against, instead of with, the Lord in my environment, which affected those around me.

The reformed complainer

THE MIRACLE OF GRATITUDE

I am happy to say that I am a recovering complainer. And now that I know better, the Holy Spirit is helping me to avoid complaining by helping me set up safeguards to avoid reinfection. To avoid reinfection, here is my secret: Whenever I am walking towards a group of people who are deep in conversation, the Lord prompts me to study their faces. If any of the faces in the group has a certain "look," it tells me that there is a small chance of infection, and I should tread carefully. Now, if more than a third of the group have this "look," there is a high chance of infection, and I should steer clear. If more than half of the group have this "look" on their faces, the level of infection is at the highest levels of contagion. Then I know I should consider exiting the building immediately. Do I hear you ask, "What is the "look?" That look is what I would like to call, " lemon face."

"Lemon face" is the facial expression we get when we eat something really sour like a lemon. Therefore, "lemon face" is the face people make when they are tasting the sour fruit of complaining and pretending they don't like it even though they are having a great time. If you stand in front of the mirror and pretend you are eating lemons, you can recreate the face. Yes, lemon face is the key to my success. Every time, the Holy Spirit helps me recognize the "lemon face" look, I steer clear of the environment. So, if we happen to be in the same place and, while walking toward your group, I suddenly make a beeline for the exit, it may be that I have seen some facial expressions that are worrisome. And I may be wrong. It may be that your discussion group really is eating lemons, not complaining. However, complaining is so toxic to the Holy Spirit's work in my life that I am no longer willing to take any chances.

Instead of "lemon face," I use "bone face"

Avoiding complaining is especially hard at work, where people tend to complain about everything; but the Lord is also helping me in that space as well. When I find myself in that unproductive space of complaining at work in which no real work is being done, the Holy Spirit has given me a strategy to make a face, known when I was growing up in Nigeria as "bone face."

For those of you who are unfamiliar, "bone face" is a blank facial expression that betrays no emotion and shows no empathy. Bone face may have been the expression that Isaiah was describing in Isaiah 50:7 when he said, "I have set my face like a flint." Bone face discourages a person from continuing in the complaint. For example, they may say, "The way they treat women in this place is ridiculous." And I stand there and do bone face. Or they say, "Can you imagine how low our salaries are . . . ?" Bone face! "They work us like dogs. . . ." Bone face! No matter the complaint, I just stand there and do bone face.

Since I stopped joining people in their complaining, the Lord has taken away many of those situations that I would otherwise complain about: He has lifted me to a place of respect; He has increased my pay; and He has stopped me from working like a dog. So even though I never had anything to complain about in the first place, He has now physically removed all my reasons to complain. So, I choose to no longer be identified as a complainer. And, to avoid being infected with complaining, I do what Isaiah suggests and "set my face like a flint" (bone face!)

Inevitably, I don't have as many friends at work as I used to. And the ones with whom I used to sit and complain, for whom our complaining habit was ingrained, the Lord has transferred them to other places, far away from me. So, now that I stay away from constant reinfection, I am able to successfully avoid complaining.

So, I have now shared with you the strategies the Lord gives me to help me avoid complaining. I want you to use some of these strategies for yourself as well. As you go forward from this chapter, I invite you to choose not to complain any more. I also invite you to avoid any spaces in which people gather to complain. If you accept my invitation and make the commitment to avoid complaining, it is going to seem hard at first. But as you practice gratitude instead of complaining, the Holy Spirit will help you. Let's pray together:

"Father, please help your children avoid complaining. Set up safeguards around them and connect them with others who are like-minded who will help them enter into the dimensions of gratitude." Amen.

THE SUB-ZERO DIMENSION

Let's move on to the dimensions

Wow, I spent a long time discussing the sub-zero dimension of complaining, which is not what this book is about. However, I needed to take the time to explain it because it is a hidden dimension that could negatively impact your walking in the miracles of gratitude. I wanted to show you the insidious nature of the sub-zero dimension so that you would recognize its power to prevent you from advancing from the first to the second and, eventually, to the third dimension of gratitude. No matter how far you come in any of the dimensions of gratitude that I am about to reveal to you, the anti-miracle math of the sub-zero dimension will always prevail. Therefore, please stay away from complaining.

I am confident that you now understand how to avoid the sub-zero dimension of complaining. So, let's move on to discuss the actual dimensions of gratitude, starting with the first dimension.

First Dimension Gratitude

12 Now when he was in affliction, he implored the Lord his God, and humbled himself greatly before the God of his fathers, 13 and prayed to Him; and He received his entreaty, heard his supplication, and brought him back to Jerusalem into his kingdom. Then Manasseh knew that the Lord was God (II Chronicles, 33:12-13).

An aborted landing

It was nearing 8:00 pm and we had been in the plane, sitting on the tarmac, for over an hour. However, the captain's voice sounded confident as it reached us over the intercom. He apologized for the delay and assured us that our flight would soon take off. The flight deck was taking all the necessary precautions to chart a safe flight path to our destination. Very soon, they would have all the details worked out and we would be on our way.

I looked out of the window as the rain beat down on the airport. With predicted winds of up to fifty-five miles per hour, Hurricane Ian was nearing my home city, and I was convinced that the flight should have been cancelled. A cancellation notice had been sent for my earlier flight, which had not surprised me. However, I was surprised that the later flight, which I was now on, was approved for takeoff. I reassured myself that the pilot knew what he was doing and that he would not take off if he was not convinced he could get us to our destination safely. Having convinced myself that all was well, I settled into my work. My job was to finish working on a proposal while the pilot's job was to fly the plane.

But as we took off into the night sky, all was not well. The captain had promised some turbulence; but what we were experiencing was bad. It was as if were in a cyclone riding a bucking horse without reins. The pilot had sounded confident; but now I was not so sure he had a handle on the situation. I tried to ignore the shaking plane and reassured myself again. I had been working on a project that gave me a sense of purpose such that I was confident the plane could not crash; however, things did not look promising. I gripped my seat.

As we made our descent for the landing, it was clear that something was wrong. The twenty-four tons of our Embraer jet lunged as if we were in a roller coaster. But this was no roller coaster − we were over 10,000 feet in the air! It was beginning to dawn on my untrained pilot mind that we could not overcome the force of the winds. A safe landing was not guaranteed.

The gravity of the situation was obvious, but it went unspoken among the passengers. Instead, we communicated it to each other in the deathly silence that hung over the entire cabin. Given the situation, I was impressed that everyone was so quiet. But then the plane lunged once more; and, this time, someone screamed.

THE MIRACLE OF GRATITUDE

After what seemed like an eternity, the captain's voice was heard over the intercom. He confirmed our suspicions: Just seconds from the ground, our landing had been aborted. Our rising altitude was the sign that our trajectory had been altered. Our plane was now being diverted to another airport.

Although the turbulence was still rough, the change in the cabin's atmosphere was palpable. Over seventy passengers breathed a huge sigh of relief as we turned away from the hurricane, toward a new destination, and a safer landing. But it was not until twelve hours, 953 miles, and two flights later that I finally arrived at my intended destination. As I debriefed the experience with my fellow passengers, we all felt grateful to be alive.

My fellow passengers and I had just come through a near miss experience, which led us to express first dimension gratitude.

Gratitude of the "near miss" experience

First dimension gratitude is the gratitude that comes out of a near miss experience. It is birthed in dire situations, such as a major car crash, in which you barely escape with your life. In first dimension gratitude, you know it was the Lord who saved you. The Lord's intervention is obvious because you are still alive when you didn't expect to be. So, first dimension gratitude comes from a salvation experience that is so clear, you practically need to be sleeping or unconscious to miss what the Lord did. The hand of the Lord was so clear in the situation; you didn't need to be a Christian to call it. Everybody, including the people who say they don't believe in God, can testify that what occurred was a supernatural intervention.

A supernatural intervention is a common precipitator of first dimension gratitude. An example is seen in the story of Israel when they witnessed Elijah's burnt offering being consumed by fire from heaven (1 Kings 18:38). The onlookers were so impressed with this obviously supernatural event that they fell on their faces and exclaimed, "The Lord, He is God! The Lord, He is God!" In first dimension gratitude, people easily recognize the Lord's move because He literally comes down from heaven and slaps the people with His greatness. And like people waking up from a deep sleep, those present see His mighty hand and say, "Oh yeah. Wow! Look at what God did."

These types of salvation experiences are rare; therefore, people living only in first dimension gratitude don't get many chances to say, "Thank you." The threshold level at which they notice the Lord's goodness is so high that they rarely see what the Lord is doing. If the Lord does not demonstrate His power by doing a miracle, sending fire down from heaven, or raising the dead, they don't feel like much has happened. For this reason, their "thank yous" are not many.

People who only express first dimension gratitude don't feel that they owe the Lord much. They don't see the Lord doing much in their lives, so they don't feel the need to go out of their way to thank Him except, of course, on special occasions. For this reason, people who only express first dimension gratitude tend to attend church services no more than once or twice a year, primarily during major Christian holidays such as Easter. And then, they gather en masse with believers and unbelievers alike to say an obligatory "thank you." Thank you" is heard so rarely from people who stay in first dimension gratitude because they don't get to experience many miracles in their lives. The absence of miracles in their lives is a result of first dimension math.

First dimension gratitude produces miracles of multiplication by one

The math of first dimension gratitude is the simple math of multiplying by 1. Let's practice this math now. What do you get when you multiply any number by 1? Correct! You will always get the same number back. Whatever you multiply by one is what you get. Now, let's do a few math problems. What is 1x1? How about 1 x 35? Ok, now 1 x 3 million? Excellent. You recognize that every time you multiply a number by 1, you will always end up with the same number you started with.

These math problems help us understand the miracles that arise from first dimension gratitude because what you get is what you started with. Therefore, in first dimension gratitude, you get what you get. If you are in a near miss situation in which you almost get killed in a car crash, but you survive and then show gratitude, that first dimension gratitude gives you the miracle of your life. If, after eight years of struggling through college, you finally graduate and only then show gratitude, first dimension gratitude allows you to keep (use) your college degree. If you are almost wrongfully convicted for a crime you didn't commit and only after your exoneration do you show gratitude, then that expression of first dimension gratitude helps you keep your freedom. In these examples, we see that first dimension gratitude gives you back the very thing for which you show gratitude. Therefore, in first dimension gratitude, what you see is what you get.

The minimum level of gratitude

The reason first dimension gratitude does not produce many miracles is because it represents a minimum level of gratitude. Therefore, it carries with it minimum creative power. A minimum level of creative power occurs because a minimally thankful person speaks very few "spirit words" of gratitude and therefore, creates very few things. Also, when a person is not often thankful, the chances are high that they spend at least some of their time in the sub-zero dimension of complaining. So, the complaining/minimal gratitude cycle often reduces what miracles have previously been created to zero. At this minimum level of gratitude, the absence of creative power is a problem for Heaven (here representing the Lord and His angels).

THE MIRACLE OF GRATITUDE

Heaven has a quota for what it expects to come from our lives. Because we are people with a God-given purpose, Heaven expects that our lives will be lived to the praise of God's glory. When the gratitude that comes from our lives is minimal, it is as if Heaven is scraping the bottom of our gratitude barrels. Although we may feel as if we are doing great, Heaven is not impressed. In this minimal state of gratitude, we are barely making a passing grade. Perhaps this situation might be better clarified if we try to see things from Heaven's perspective.

Suppose Heaven has been orchestrating so much goodness in someone's life, but Heaven only hears from them when they visit the church on special occasions like Christmas and Easter. Heaven has been saving that person's life every day but only hears from them once in a while when they get out of trouble. Heaven is looking at the record of that person's gratitude; but the record is bare. Their gratitude is only measurable on the scale during Thanksgiving; but it quickly drops back to zero after Black Friday, then rises slightly at Christmas, but only if they received good gifts. You can see that this minimal level of gratitude falls short of how much goodness they have received.

This person's minimal level of gratitude is a problem for Heaven because Heaven cannot easily justify that person's existence. A minimal level of gratitude is a sign to Heaven that a person is no longer producing fruit. Our ability to produce fruit is critical to fulfilling our God-given mandate on earth (John 15:16). Therefore, fruitlessness is a real problem.

Heaven's problem with fruitlessness is demonstrated in the story of the fig tree in Luke 13:6-9:

> *6 He also spoke this parable: "A certain man had a fig tree planted in his vineyard, and he came seeking fruit on it and found none. 7 Then he said to the keeper of his vineyard, 'Look, for three years I have come seeking fruit on this fig tree and find none. Cut it down; why does it use up the ground?' 8 But he answered and said to him, 'Sir, let it alone this year also, until I dig around it and fertilize it. 9 And if it bears fruit, well. But if not, after that you can cut it down.'*

In the above scripture, the owner of the vineyard is upset with the fig tree because it is not producing fruit. For this reason, He is ready to cut down the tree.

Every vineyard owner has an expectation of fruit. In John 15:16, the Lord is clear about His expectation that we will produce fruit because by producing fruit, we bring Him glory. So, when our lives lack evidence of the fruit of creative power that is released through gratitude, God does not get the glory. If God cannot be glorified through a person's life, like the parable of the fig tree, it becomes difficult to justify their existence.

In this parable, however, you may notice that there is an Intercessor pleading on the fig tree's behalf. This Intercessor says, "Let's see if this fig tree will bear fruit after I take some extraordinary measures" (*my paraphrase*). It is as if the Intercessor is saying, "Let's do some obvious miracles in this life and see if we can activate some gratitude." Therefore, extra special and mighty miracles are sent from Heaven to get their attention to see if, perhaps, that person will express some first dimension gratitude.

If the plan works and the person's spirit expresses the minimum level of gratitude acceptable to Heaven, then they get to keep their lives; because the sentence of "cutting down the tree" is commuted. For this reason, first dimension gratitude only gives you back your life. A person's coming to church three times a year may keep them alive, which is a big deal, but it doesn't get them much more than that.

Manasseh's experience with first dimension gratitude

We see an example of first dimension gratitude in 2 Chronicles 33 in the life of King Manasseh, son of King Hezekiah. Having King Hezekiah for a dad in those days would be comparable in our days to being a "pastor's kid." See, not only was Hezekiah a king, but He was also a man who followed the Lord. In fact, Hezekiah walked closely with the Lord such that it would be hard for His family to miss the relationship. None of Hezekiah's children, and certainly not Manasseh, could legitimately pretend that they did not know of the Lord's existence. They might be able to feign indifference; but they could not honestly say they were not aware of the Lord's presence in their home. Therefore, it is likely that

FIRST DIMENSION GRATITUDE

Manasseh had personal experience of his father's relationship with the Lord.

Manasseh's father, Hezekiah, was a king who handed over all his problems to the Lord. Once, when Sennacherib, king of Assyria, wrote him a threatening letter, Hezekiah took the letter to "church" and presented it before the Lord (II Kings 19:14). Unfortunately for Sennacherib, the Lord accepted the letter as if it had been written personally to Him. Before Sennacherib could understand what he was up against, he experienced the Lord's power against him. All the mighty men, leaders, and captains of his army were slain overnight by the angel of the Lord (2 Kings 19:35). Thus, Hezekiah's trust of the Lord proved to be Sennacherib's undoing.

Hezekiah also had a direct line of access to the Lord, which was not common in those days. A day came when Hezekiah received a visit from the prophet Isaiah (2 Kings 20: 1). Isaiah told Hezekiah to settle his affairs because Hezekiah would soon die. However, as Isaiah was leaving Hezekiah's room, Hezekiah immediately dialed in to Heaven to ask for healing from the Lord. The Lord instantly granted Hezekiah's request and lengthened his life. Meanwhile, Isaiah, who should have been the first to know what was happening, was asked to go back and rescind his prophecy (2 Kings 20:4-5). These powerful experiences, which marked Hezekiah's life, would have been known to any member of Hezekiah's family.

THE MIRACLE OF GRATITUDE

Given Hezekiah's history with the Lord, it seems surprising that Manasseh chose a different path. Instead of serving the Lord, Manasseh chose instead to turn away from and live out his life in opposition to the Lord (2 Chronicles 33). And Manasseh was not content to be indifferent or neutral. He chose to go all the way to the left of his father to be super evil. Thus, Manasseh set his mind to do evil things, including serve idols, desecrate the temple, practice witchcraft, and sacrifice his children to demons. Manasseh did so much evil in the sight of the Lord, that he provoked the Lord to anger.

Let's read about the Lord's reaction in 2 Chronicles 33:10-13

> *10 And the Lord spoke to Manasseh and his people, but they would not listen. 11 Therefore the Lord brought upon them the captains of the army of the king of Assyria, who took Manasseh with hooks, bound him with bronze fetters, and carried him off to Babylon. 12 Now when he was in affliction, he implored the Lord his God, and humbled himself greatly before the God of his fathers, 13 and prayed to Him; and He received his entreaty, heard his supplication, and brought him back to Jerusalem into his kingdom. Then Manasseh knew that the Lord was God.*

It was not until Manasseh found himself in trouble that he remembered the Lord. There, in the affliction of prison with hooks in his nose and chains around his feet, Manasseh came to his senses. He prayed to the Lord God of his father, Hezekiah, and repented. And the Lord, who is loving and kind and always waiting for us to turn back to Him, saved Manasseh and brought him back to his kingdom. It was at this point that Manasseh acknowledged the Lord's goodness.

It was only after the Lord's great deliverance that Manasseh demonstrated first dimension gratitude. And Manasseh's expression of first dimension gratitude was rewarded with the miracle of his salvation. Thus, Manasseh's story is the perfect picture of a life lived only in first dimension gratitude.

The bump in the road

Like Manasseh, many of us live lives that are independent of the Lord because we feel that we can get along well without Him. So, we do what we want, live as we like, and sometimes even go against the Lord's principles. Like Manasseh, we may thrive for a season, which might embolden us to stray further from the Lord or do more things that are displeasing to Him. But somewhere, deep down in our hearts, we know the truth. We know that He is not pleased with us, and we can feel the separation from His Spirit. When we allow ourselves to connect with our spirit, we can tell that something is deeply wrong.

But not everyone responds appropriately to their bad feelings. For some people, that bad feeling is medicated with drugs, thrills, or living life in the fast lane, trying, unsuccessfully, to drown out the Lord's pull of conviction. For others, the bad feeling is medicated with intermittent "shots" of first dimension gratitude, including doing things like going to church occasionally, giving money to charity, or sometimes turning down an opportunity for egregious sin. Unlike the former group that is at risk of losing any chance at repentance (Proverbs 29:1), this latter group's intermittent expressions of first dimension gratitude can keep them going long enough to give them a chance to repent. But eventually, all people who live like Manasseh will hit the bump in the road.

The bump in the road is the pivotal experience that brings down our carefully constructed house of cards. It is the thing that happens that reminds us that we are nothing without the Lord. For some people, instead of a major bump, there are several mini bumps, such as the near miss car crash that brings them back to church, or the heart attack that sets them back on the straight and narrow. But for all who continue to live a life of minimal fruitfulness, there comes a major bump in the road such as the one Manasseh experienced. This bump in the road forces a decision point at which people have to decide whether to continue to live without the Lord or seek His forgiveness and return to Him.

If we choose to return to the Lord, we will find, as Manasseh experienced, that the Lord is quick to forgive and restore us to relationship with Him. But the decision is really up to us. We can choose to turn to Him and recognize the abundance of His goodness in our lives or we can decide to continue to live without the Lord, which hurts us.

FIRST DIMENSION GRATITUDE

If we choose to live apart from the Lord or intermittently show up to express first dimension gratitude, it hurts us because we cannot partner with the Lord to create good in our environments. Therefore, we and those in our immediate environment experience a life lived apart from the Lord as scarcity.

This scarcity may not show up as obvious poverty. In fact, like Manasseh, many people living apart from the Lord have great status and wealth. They look like they have money, property, influence, and popularity; but they lack the abundance that only comes through partnering with the Lord. Instead of the fruit of righteousness, including love, joy, peace, kindness, and self-control (Galatians 5:22-23), they live with anxiety, fear, and violence (Ezekiel 12:19). Therefore, although people who don't care for the Lord may appear as if they are "rich," from the Lord's perspective, they are worse than poor. They are, in fact, wretched, miserable, blind, and naked.

Hear what the Lord says about them in the Book of Revelation:

> *Because you say, 'I am rich, have become wealthy, and have need of nothing'—and do not know that you are wretched, miserable, poor, blind, and naked* (Revelation 3:17)

Therefore, the Lord issues a mandate to them as follows:

> *I counsel you to buy from Me gold refined in the fire, that you may be rich; and white garments, that you may be clothed, that the shame of*

THE MIRACLE OF GRATITUDE

your nakedness may not be revealed; and anoint your eyes with eye salve, that you may see (Revelation 3:18).

Did you notice that the Lord points out their blindness? This blindness is the main reason why some people live in their lives in first dimension gratitude only. Because they cannot see what the Lord is doing all around them, they struggle to show gratitude. And because they lack gratitude, their scarce "spirit words" create very little. Thus, people who are blind to the Lord's abundant provision produce little and are at risk for losing even what little they have.

An example of the effects of the blindness of living in first dimension gratitude only is shown in the Parable of the Talents (Matthew 25:14-30). In this story, a man delivers talents (money) to his servants before embarking on a long journey. To the first servant, he gives five talents; to the second two talents; and to the third, one talent. In their master's absence, the first servant with the five talents doubles his earnings to ten. Likewise, the servant who received two talents doubled his earnings to four. But the third servant produced nothing more than he already had.

When asked to give an account of his business dealings, the third servant gave a report that highlighted his scarcity mindset. Instead of seeing his master gift as an act of generosity, he could only see stinginess. Instead of seeing business opportunity, he was fearful that the money would be stolen. And so, instead of partnering with his master to produce more wealth, he decided instead to dig a hole in the ground and hide the money. This servant produced nothing. And the end result of his lack of productivity (unfruitfulness) is that the little he did have was taken away.

His experience is summed up as follows:

> *29 'For to everyone who has, more will be given, and he will have abundance; but from him who does not have, even what he has will be taken away . . ."* (Matthew 25:29)

We need acknowledge what we have by showing gratitude, which leads us to create more of what we already have. But if we don't acknowledge our abundance by sowing seeds of gratitude, even the little we do have will be taken away from us.

Live a life of consistent gratitude

If we are to live lives that are pleasing to the Lord, we must start paying more attention to His abundance in our lives and showing gratitude for it. Living in a state of consistent gratitude helps us partner with the Lord to create an environment filled with His goodness.

I invite you to choose today to pay close attention to what the Lord is doing for you every day. Choose not to wait for big events in your life to show Him gratitude. Choose instead to show gratitude for the small things in your life. As we practice consistent gratitude, our power to create good in our environments becomes magnified.

THE MIRACLE OF GRATITUDE

Maintaining a consistent level of gratitude allows us to move from first dimension only gratitude to unleash the miracles of second dimension gratitude.

Second Dimension Gratitude

¹²Then Isaac sowed in that land, and reaped in the same year a hundredfold; and the Lord blessed him. ¹³The man began to prosper, and continued prospering until he became very prosperous; ¹⁴for he had possessions of flocks and possessions of herds and a great number of servants. So the Philistines envied him. (Genesis 26:12-14)

The money came out of nowhere

I looked at the bank balance and did a double take. The numbers surprised me. Surely they were wrong. I signed out of the banking app and signed back in. No, it was real. The balance had substantially increased, and it made no sense. Surely, there had been a mistake. I checked with Chiedu, and he was just as surprised. From where did the extra money come? It made no sense to celebrate. Why celebrate a mistake? If it was a mistake, as we were sure it was, it was only a matter of time before someone discovered it and requested a full refund. We needed to get to the bottom of this mystery, fast.

To investigate, I went through my paystubs and found it. The mystery line item read "bonus." Hmmm, bonus. What bonus? No one had said anything about a bonus. I was not expecting a bonus. This was not even the season for a bonus. The season for bonuses had passed and I had already received mine. Therefore, I was perplexed. There had been no discussion about an extra bonus. Surely, something was wrong, and I needed to sort it out because I figured that someone else was looking for lost money.

But the more I investigated, the more it seemed legitimate. A legitimate but substantial bonus had been paid into my bank account without my foreknowledge. But what had I done to deserve it? I reached out to my supervisor and asked for an explanation. He told me it was a bona fide bonus that was due to me that year for my extra work. Extra work? Really? I didn't do any extra work. Yeah I worked hard. But that was every year. In fact, since I took the job, the previous year had been the one in which I had worked the least. It was also the least stressful year on record. In honestly reviewing my effort, I thought, "Have I actually been paid more for working less?" Yes, it was the truth. Somehow, I had worked less and managed to make more. It was then that I acknowledged that the bonus was a special gift from the Lord. And I got on my knees and thanked Him for it.

About ten years earlier, when I started this new job, by national benchmarks, I was one of the lowest paid people in my role. Although we felt the Lord's leading in taking the job, the low salary hurt. Our cross-country move had upended Chiedu's job, leaving him looking for a new one. We had not been able to sell our home because the mortgage was underwater (we owed more on the home than it was worth) so, we were paying for two homes at the same time (ouch!). At the same time, my student loan deferrals had run out and the debt had come due. We had day care expenses, and we needed to front money for appliances (the new place had no washer or dryer). To put it mildly, our finances were tenuous, and the low salary did not help.

So, for the first six months of this new role, we went into debt to make ends meet. At the end of the month, we had more expenses than we had income. The math did not work. Every month the paycheck came, instead of growing, our bank balance got smaller. And since we had no reserves, we were making ends meet with borrowed money. It was not until six months later that Chiedu's new job started us on the journey of climbing out of debt.

Slowly, but surely, over years of penny pinching with God's favor on our finances, our debt was eliminated. I also entered into salary negotiations at work, which also raised our income. At the same time, the Lord rearranged my work schedule such that work became easier and my work-associated stress substantially decreased. So, I was working a better schedule with less stress and more pay. The transformation was unreal. But the Lord had promised that it would occur and all that happened was consistent with the Lord fulfilling His promises.

The Lord's promise had come to us at a time when I discovered how low my salary was relative to most people at my job. When I did the math of how much income should have come to me if I had made the right salary from the start, I wrote it down and showed it to my supervisor. I told them that they owed me back pay. I was told then that "rightsizing" my salary would take many years and that it would not be possible to receive any back pay. But we didn't take the man's word as the law. Instead, we presented the matter before the Lord. And the word of the Lord came to us that we would recover all. And we held fast to His word and thanked Him for His promise. Even though we could not see it, we thanked Him. Even when the years went by with no change in our situation, we believed His word and we thanked Him in advance for His supernatural provision.

In a matter of years, the Lord turned our finances around. He supernaturally accelerated our debt. He rearranged our work schedules so that we worked less and had more time. He also dramatically increased our income and started sending us random bonuses. Even when people would declare that there was no money, the Lord would create a new scenario to get it to us. People were reluctantly releasing money to us, and it was clearly the Lord's doing in fulfillment of His word. Hence, our random but legitimate bonus at the beginning of this story was part of His promise fulfillment.

As the Lord's financial surprises continue to unfold, we are grateful, and we celebrate His goodness. He moved us from being bank financiers (we are certain we helped finance our bank's new furniture), to kingdom financiers. And He doesn't stop; He

54

continues to send His rain of financial blessings. Even when we feel that we have more than enough, He surprises us again and again. All we can do is to cry out at God's undeserved grace and mercy.

So, the mystery of the new bank balance was solved. The bonus check was sent by the Lord through human agents who, though they had no idea what was happening, were working in accordance with the Lord's will. Although the blessing could not easily be explained by human standards, we saw that the Lord was simply showing us another dimension of His incredible provision.

In this experience, we walked through a miracle of second dimension gratitude.

Gratitude for all that we see

Second dimension gratitude is gratitude we express for the many things that the Lord has done, as we become aware of them. Therefore, second dimension gratitude is "See it first" gratitude. You see it and then you thank the Lord for it.

Second dimension gratitude is different from first dimension gratitude because it thanks the Lord for all things, both little and big. Unlike first dimension gratitude, which waits for a testimony-worthy act of God to show gratitude, second dimension gratitude shows gratitude for anything and everything the Lord has done. People who practice second dimension gratitude are always looking for and paying attention to what the Lord is doing; for this reason, they will always find something to be thankful for.

Second dimension gratitude is gratitude for anything from the incredible and supernatural to the esoteric and mundane. It is gratitude for salvation and healing; but also, gratitude for daily life and a functioning body. It is gratitude for the air we breathe, but also, gratitude for our ability to breathe that air. Second dimension gratitude is gratitude for the sun, the moon, and the stars, but also, gratitude for parents, siblings, and children. It is gratitude for a salary and paycheck, but also, gratitude for the ability to show up at work and carry out tasks. Second dimension gratitude is grateful for anything that can be seen, felt, and experienced.

Second dimension gratitude is the place that gracious people occupy. People who practice second dimension gratitude will usually find reasons to thank people where no clear reason exists. They'll thank people for showing up, being present, and involved. They'll thank people for taking their call, talking with them, and answering their questions. They'll thank people for their time, energy, and effort. They tend to be people who tip generously. People who walk in second dimension gratitude always find reasons to show their gratitude.

People who practice second dimension gratitude might even show gratitude for unusual things. They might show gratitude for both animate and inanimate things. They might show gratitude for their pets, their cars, or their shoes. They might show gratitude for the sun, moon, and trees. They might show gratitude for their computers and phones. People who live in second dimension gratitude will thank anyone and anything at any time and for everything. And they express gratitude consistently because they have unlocked the dimension's miracle math.

Second dimension gratitude produces miracles of exponential increase

Unlike the math of the sub-zero (multiplying by 0) and first dimensions (multiplying by 1), second dimension math is difficult to do in one's head. It can even be difficult to do using pen and paper. To do second dimension math, you often need a calculator because it is about multiplying numbers by themselves several times over. The math of second dimension gratitude activates miracles using the math of exponents.

Exponents tell us how many times a number should be multiplied by itself. If we take, for example, 2^2, we understand that we should multiply two by itself two times over: $2 \times 2 = 4$. If we need to solve the problem, 2^4, we understand that we should multiply two by itself four times over: $2 \times 2 \times 2 \times 2 = 16$. These examples are easy to do because the numbers are small; however, as we work our way to higher numbers, our math brain struggles. For example, what is two to the power 56 (2^{56})? How about 15^{75}? Exactly! Multiplying using exponential forms is hard.

THE MIRACLE OF GRATITUDE

The point of these math problems is not to stress you out; but to help you recognize that second dimension math is hard because the numbers increase exponentially. Therefore, second dimension gratitude causes exponential increase. When we practice second dimension gratitude, the things for which we show gratitude increase exponentially.

Second dimension gratitude will always lead to exponential increase. When we express gratitude for our food, we find that the Lord's provision increases exponentially (Mark 6:41-44). When we express gratitude for life, we experience a richer, more vibrant life than we had previously (John 11:41-44). When we express gratitude for our health, we experience the Lord's gift of wholeness (Luke 17:15, 18-19). When we show gratitude for our children, they thrive and enter into destiny (Psalms 144:12). When we show gratitude for what we are learning, our level of understanding increases even more (Luke 10:21). Thus, second dimension gratitude expands the things for which we show gratitude.

Second dimension math works the same, whether our gratitude is expressed to the Lord or to people. We have already seen that gratitude expressed to the Lord brings us more of what we are grateful for (John 6:11). But it works the same with people. People are also likely to produce more of the thing for which they are shown gratitude. When we show gratitude to someone who came to visit, it encourages them to come again. When we show gratitude to someone who cooks us a delicious meal, they are more

58

likely to invite us back for more. When we show gratitude to our children for giving us hugs, they are more likely to hug us more. When we show gratitude to a server for giving us great service, they are more likely to serve us more enthusiastically. People tend to produce more of what we show them gratitude for.

Second dimension principles also apply to our environment. When we show gratitude for the sunshine, we tend to experience more of sunshine. When we show gratitude for the sound of birds chirping in the trees, we tend to hear them more often and their chirping becomes more noticeable and sweeter. When we show gratitude for the trees and the shade they provide, more opportunities seem to arise for us to enjoy their shade. Wherever it is expressed, second dimension gratitude creates opportunities for more gratitude.

She showed second dimension gratitude

An example of second dimension gratitude is seen in the life of Deborah (Judges 5), one of Israel's judges. Deborah was a prophetess who had prophesied that Barak, the captain of Israel's army, would win a victory over Sisera, the commander of the enemy army that was under the leadership Jabin, King of Canaan. The battle that Barak fought against Sisera was the first in a series of battles that would eventually be fought to overthrow Jabin's regime (Judges 4:24). Yet, at the end of their first victory, Deborah and Barak took time to celebrate the Lord's deliverance (Judges 5).

Rather than wait until all the battles had been fought and won, Barak and Deborah chose to celebrate their nascent victory immediately. Instead of bemoaning how many more battles would be needed to clinch the victory, they celebrated how far they had come. They composed a song to the Lord that their gratitude for His amazing deliverance. By celebrating one victory, they activated more wins, which led them to lead a successful revolt against Jabin until they overthrew his oppressive leadership.

Second dimension gratitude enhances our vision

Not only does second dimension gratitude reproduce more of what we see and show gratitude for, but it also enhances what we see and shows us a more nuanced version of what previously existed. By enhancing our vision, second dimension gratitude allows the Lord to give us insight by showing us a new and dynamic perspective of something we previously thought we understood but didn't fully grasp. Let's take as an example, the rain.

The rain is a weather phenomenon that very few people, except, perhaps, farmers, are grateful for. In fact, people tend to think about the rain in a somewhat negative light. This negative perception of rain shows up in common phrases like "It rained on my parade," or in nursery rhymes like, "Rain, rain, go away . . . !" Most of the time, the rain gets bad press.

It may be safe to say that, other than farmers, most people do not welcome the rain. People planning an outside event would prefer

SECOND DIMENSION GRATITUDE

to have no rain. Where I come from, many women who have spent hours and good money getting their hair blow dried do not appreciate the rain or even any hint of water (humidity) in the atmosphere. Most people don't appreciate the rain because they don't understand the rain. However, people who understand second dimension gratitude (and farmers) totally get the rain.

See, rain is a prophetic pronouncement of the future. Rain is the check written by heaven that the earth cashes in to deliver the harvest. As drops of rain fall from the sky, they bring nourishment to the fields, which guarantees the harvest. As rain falls from the sky, the rivers and streams are replenished, causing an increased stock of fish for food. As rain falls from the sky, the meadows are lush, the trees blossom, and the green landscape bring us opportunities for peaceful picnics. Therefore, when you demonstrate gratitude for the rain, we actually look beyond the rain to show gratitude for everything that is a downstream effect of the rain. So, not only does gratitude for the rain produce exponential increase in the rain, but it also produces an exponential increase of the things that arise because of that rain.

Therefore, people who show second dimension gratitude for the rain receive much more than just more rainy days. They also receive more food, fuller waterways, more fish varieties, more beautiful flowers, more verdant grasslands, more peaceful environments, and more opportunities to grow in community.

THE MIRACLE OF GRATITUDE

The rain is only one example of the many gifts that can come out of second dimension gratitude. Think about how showing gratitude for the onset of a menstrual period can bring forth unborn generations. Think about how a kindergarten teacher, who shows gratitude for her rowdy class, may really be birthing the next generation of new inventions and innovative businesses. Think about how one pastor showing gratitude for his small Bible study may actually be producing many church plants down the road. Because exponential growth is unfathomable, second dimension gratitude will always bring much more than we originally bargained for. Second dimension gratitude will also bring us new innovations than we can link to the original thing for which we are grateful.

Given all the goodness that comes with second dimension gratitude, people who do not show second dimension gratitude also miss out on more than they bargained for. This example is illustrated by a story in in Luke 17:11-19.

> *11 Now it happened as He went to Jerusalem that He passed through the midst of Samaria and Galilee. 12 Then as He entered a certain village, there met Him ten men who were lepers, who stood afar off. 13 And they lifted up their voices and said, "Jesus, Master, have mercy on us!" 14 So when He saw them, He said to them, "Go, show yourselves to the priests." And so it was that as they went, they were cleansed. 15 And one of them, when he saw that he was healed, returned, and with a loud voice glorified God, 16 and fell down on his*

SECOND DIMENSION GRATITUDE

face at His feet, giving Him thanks. And he was a Samaritan. ¹⁷ So Jesus answered and said, "Were there not ten cleansed? But where are the nine? ¹⁸ Were there not any found who returned to give glory to God except this foreigner?" ¹⁹ And He said to him, "Arise, go your way. Your faith has made you well."

From the above scripture, we see that ten people came to the Lord Jesus with a medical problem (leprosy), from which the Lord Jesus healed them. However, their healing was not discovered until they were on their way to show themselves to the priest. Their healing from leprosy was a big deal because it was their ticket to escaping the shame and stigma associated with their disease. From now on, they would no longer be seen as outcasts. They could be reunited with their families and be seen in social circles once more. So, this healing was a big deal.

The one problem with the healing is that it happened away from the healer. If they had been in the presence of Jesus when the healing occurred, it would have been easy to show gratitude right away. However, now, they would need to go out of their way to go back to Jesus to say, "Thank you." Ten people pondered this challenge and, for many reasons, nine decided that the return trip to the Lord Jesus was not needed. Perhaps some thought, "He's the Lord. He should know I am grateful." Others may have felt that their long-awaited family reunion was more important. Still, others may have had important matters to settle quickly. Whatever their reasons, what we know is that nine of them missed an opportunity to show gratitude.

But one person, the outsider – a Samaritan – made a different choice. He recognized that the Lord Jesus was the source of his healing and, therefore, deserved his gratitude. So, he made the return journey. The journey was probably long and hard; otherwise, more people would have made it. But he was the only one to return to the Lord Jesus to express his gratitude.

Seeing him alone, the Lord Jesus was disappointed. He was grieved that only one person had come back to show gratitude. Perhaps if the nine had just shown a little gratitude, then He could have blessed them with more. Unfortunately, they were nowhere to be found. They got what they wanted; but they may have missed out on more.

These nine had experienced the healing of their skin condition; but they likely had more needs that the Lord could have met. Unfortunately, they never got a chance to find out. While healing was one of the many blessings the Lord Jesus could bestow, there was much more that He could gift to them. Perhaps He wanted to bless their new careers or pray over the people they would marry or the children they would have. Perhaps He also wanted to forgive their sin and give them a new mission. Maybe He wanted to change their life direction and show them a new way of living. Although we will never know for sure, it appears that their lack of gratitude prevented them from experiencing more of the Lord Jesus. And they missed out on anything else that the Lord had for them because they did not come back to express their gratitude.

The challenge with not expressing gratitude is that it can lead to the kind of "blindness" that operates in first dimension-only gratitude. Remember that, in second dimension gratitude, the more we see and acknowledge the Lord's goodness, the more of His goodness we see. The opposite is equally true. The less we see and acknowledge the Lord's goodness, the less opportunities we have to see more of what the Lord is doing.

Essentially, the fewer our episodes of second dimension gratitude, the smaller the number of second dimension miracles we experience. This negative cycle can lead to a downward spiral of blindness to the incredible things the Lord is doing. This spiritual principle is expressed in Romans 1:18-21.

> *18 For the wrath of God is revealed from heaven against all ungodliness and unrighteousness of men, who suppress the truth in unrighteousness, 19 because what may be known of God is manifest in them, for God has shown it to them. 20 For since the creation of the world His invisible attributes are clearly seen, being understood by the things that are made, even His eternal power and Godhead, so that they are without excuse, 21 because, although they knew God, they did not glorify Him as God, nor were thankful, but became futile in their thoughts, and their foolish hearts were darkened.*

THE MIRACLE OF GRATITUDE

When people do not express gratitude, their hearts become darkened. They stop seeing more of what the Lord is doing. Ultimately they downgrade themselves to first dimension-only living where they need big and obvious signs and wonders to be impressed by the Lord. These people can usually be identified by their need for signs and wonders (Matthew 16:1). They refuse to believe the Lord without them (John 4:48). However, the problem is not the absence of signs. The problem is their darkened, unbelieving hearts.

These people can also be likened to shrubs in the desert as described in Jeremiah 17:6.

> For he shall be like a shrub in the desert, And shall not see when good comes, But shall inhabit the parched places in the wilderness, In a salt land which is not inhabited.

Therefore, to avoid becoming shrubs in the desert, we need to be sensitive to the Lord's wonderful acts, which happen every day and everywhere around us. As we show Him gratitude in the little things, He will open our eyes to see more of His awesomeness.

For this reason, I invite you to practice second dimension gratitude. Thank the Lord for the rain and see more food come to your table. Thank Him for the sun and see how much clean air comes from the plants that receive the sunlight. Thank Him for the warmth you enjoy and see your heart fill with more warmth and the number and quality of your friends increase. Thank the

SECOND DIMENSION GRATITUDE

Lord for the things you see so that you can exponentially improve your vision of more things to thank Him for.

I also invite you to practice second dimension gratitude with the people in your life. Thank them for their beautiful smiles. Let them know their shoes are stylish. Tell them their skin tone is gorgeous. Second dimension gratitude is limitless in the things we can show gratitude for. Let's show gratitude to everyone around us always.

Advancing beyond second dimension gratitude

I now invite you to take some time to show the Lord some second dimension gratitude. Let's turn to the Lord and begin to thank Him for the rain, the sun, the moon, the air we breathe, and shoes we wear. Let's thank Him for our health, schools, jobs, and families. Let's thank the Lord for everything.

Wow, there is so much to thank the Lord for. And as we show Him gratitude, we give Him the opportunity to exponentially magnify His goodness in our lives.

As great as second dimension miracles are, they pale in comparison to those that come out of third dimension gratitude, which we will discuss in the next chapter.

Third Dimension Gratitude

'Ah, Lord God! Behold, You have made the heavens and the earth by Your
great power and outstretched arm. There is nothing too hard for You
(Jeremiah 32:17).

We threw a starvation praise party

It was close to the end of the semester, and we were starving. What food we had could not be cooked. For days, there had been an electrical power outage and there were no signs of power returning any time soon. We had no generator and there was a national shortage of kerosene (paraffin), so my kerosene stove was unusable. We had no money to buy cooked food and we were down to our last meal – a cup of garri (granulated cassava).

The garri was less than a cup. There wasn't enough of it to satisfy one person, but it would need to stretch to feed two. My friend Maggie and I looked at each other. We were out of options, and we knew it.

The year was 1998 and we were university students in Ogbomosho, Nigeria. We had no internet; no phone; and no prospects of letting anyone know we were starving. Maggie's family lived out of state and my family lived in another country.

THIRD DIMENSION GRATITUDE

With no prospects for another meal, the cup of garri would have to do. But just as we settled down to eat, an idea came to us – it was time for a praise party.

I don't recall whose idea it was; but we both agreed that it was the right thing to do. After all, we recognized that our Father was the source of all provision and we wanted to let Him know that He was still sovereign, even when we had no food to eat.

And so, Maggie and I began to sing praises. We clapped our hands and raised them to the King of Kings and the Lord of Lords. We shouted and danced as we thanked the One who called the universe into existence. We praised the name of the One from whom abundance flowed. We celebrated His provision and His greatness. We sang and we danced until we were satisfied that we had given Him our all. And when the praise party came to an end, we sat down to our garri, gave thanks, and ate it. The meal didn't satisfy me, and it was only midday. So, to conserve energy, I lay down on the lower bunk and went to sleep.

I awoke a few hours later to the sound of my name. A woman from my hostel was trying to get my attention. She told me that someone was looking for me. I got up and found that it was one of my Nigerian "Aunties."[6] She was carrying a tray of my (at the time)

---

[6] In Nigerian culture, any woman who is significantly older than you is your auntie.

all-time favorite food – amala and egusi soup.[7] It was unbelievable. My auntie told me that I had been on her mind, and she thought she would make me something to eat. I had only ever met this auntie once. She had never cooked for me before. That day marked her first and only visit to my hostel. In fact, since that day, I have not seen her again. But somehow, inexplicably, there she was, in living color, "randomly" bringing me my favorite food.

Maggie and I sat down to the most delicious meal ever. It was certain that the Lord Himself had cooked us this meal. Maggie and I had experienced a miracle of third dimension gratitude.

Gratitude for things unseen

Third dimension gratitude is gratitude for things "unseen." It is gratitude for things we are believing for but do not yet have. In third dimension gratitude, we show gratitude to the Lord for something we have not received. While second dimension gratitude appreciates the Lord for what is already done, third dimension gratitude appreciates the Lord for what He has not yet done and may never do. Thus, third dimension gratitude comes from a place of faith. It appreciates the Lord for His faithfulness. Third dimension gratitude says, "Thank you," even when it is not certain that the Lord will do what is requested.

---

[7] Amala is made with yam flour, while egusi soup is made with melon seeds.

THIRD DIMENSION GRATITUDE

Third dimension gratitude is ancient gratitude that has been demonstrated by past heroes of our faith. David, king of Israel, was operating in third dimension gratitude when he sat before the Lord to show gratitude for the Lord's promise to establish his kingdom forever (2 Samuel 7). From this gratitude came an unusual descendant named Jesus. Daniel was also in third dimension gratitude when he knelt before the Lord to give thanks even though he was destined for the lions' den (Daniel 6). From this gratitude came an unusual salvation experience. Third dimension gratitude was also shown by the Lord Jesus when He thanked the Lord for food that was not enough (Matthew 14). And from that gratitude came food that fed thousands. Third dimension gratitude does not worry about the circumstances at hand. Third dimension gratitude ignores what the eyes see and focuses instead on the One who cannot be seen.

Third dimension gratitude produces miracles that don't make math sense

In third dimension gratitude, we enter into the realm of crazy math. Third dimension math is math that no calculator can calculate. A math formula in third dimension gratitude is unsolvable because its results are not within the realm of possibility.

Third dimension math is explainable only by the addition of an undefined constant, "X," which cannot be assigned a value because it has the ability to assume any values. This factor could also be seen as a wildcard. In third dimension math, the wildcard is the Lord, God. And as wildcard, He can do anything He pleases – make up a miracle of his choosing and do it without regard to the laws of the universe.

Third dimension math is impossible to quantify because it is not bound to the laws that govern the natural environment. While first and second dimension math are governed by the laws of the universe, third dimension math is not. This phenomenon occurs because, like second dimension math, third dimension math produces more of what we show gratitude for. In this case, however, because the gratitude is for the Lord Himself as a being, what is produced is more of the Lord. Therefore, because third dimension gratitude is focused on something or "SomeOne" outside the earthly realm who is not bound by earthly principles, miracles produced by third dimension math are also not bound to follow the laws of the earth.

Miracles out of this world

When we express gratitude to the Lord over something that has not or may never happen, we announce to Him that He is more important than our earthly circumstance. This act of faith unleashes the Lord to go into action on our behalf to create the kind of miracle that has not yet been seen. In the moment that we exalt the Lord above our circumstances to declare Him as Master of all, He becomes like a proud Father who wants to flex His muscles to honor our act of faith.

I imagine the Lord standing up in response to our radical act of gratitude and saying to His angels, "Can you see my daughter showing me gratitude in spite of her circumstances? Can you see her exalting me above her situation? Do you see her thanking me for what she does not yet have? Now, how can I respond in a way that surpasses her expectations to produce a miracle beyond her wildest dreams?" The Lord is pleased by our third dimension gratitude because it activates Him to get creative again. And the Lord loves to create new things as He did in the beginning (Genesis 1) and still does today (Isaiah 43:19).

Thus, third dimension gratitude activates the Lord to do what has not yet been seen or imagined. It liberates Him to create something new. It allows the Lord to disregard the laws of the environment in His response to our gratitude.

Third dimension gratitude announces to the Lord, His angels, and the universe that we know who He is. It tells everyone who is listening that we know what the Lord can do. And it reaffirms our trust that He will do what is needed to glorify His name. Third dimension gratitude puts the Lord on the throne and officially invites Him to show up on earth to act on our behalf.

THE MIRACLE OF GRATITUDE

An example of third dimension gratitude is seen in the story of King Jehoshaphat when he and his people are preparing for a battle in which they are both outnumbered and outmatched:

> *21 And when he had consulted with the people, he appointed those who should sing to the Lord, and who should praise the beauty of holiness, as they went out before the army and were saying: "Praise the Lord, For His mercy endures forever." 22 Now when they began to sing and to praise, the Lord set ambushes against the people of Ammon, Moab, and Mount Seir, who had come against Judah; and they were defeated. 23 For the people of Ammon and Moab stood up against the inhabitants of Mount Seir to utterly kill and destroy them. And when they had made an end of the inhabitants of Seir, they helped to destroy one another.* (2 Chronicles 20: 21-23).

The odds were stacked against Jehoshaphat and his people. By all human standards, there was no way they could win. Nevertheless, they expressed their gratitude to the Lord as they praised the beauty of His holiness. In essence, they showed gratitude for who He is. The Lord in turn created a new kind of battle strategy – one that had not yet been seen before. To make it clear that He was the one fighting this battle, He used the enemy's own weapons against them. In the end, His people did not lift a finger to fight; but the entire enemy army was destroyed. Thus, Jehoshaphat's third dimension gratitude unleashed a new kind of victory.

THIRD DIMENSION GRATITUDE

As shown in the above story, third dimension gratitude leaves the natural and focuses on the supernatural, the realm that the Lord inhabits. Third dimension gratitude releases the Lord to show us things we have never seen before and give us experiences we have never had. Because third dimension gratitude focuses on who the Lord is, it liberates him to show up as the Lord, Master of the Universe. Therefore, third dimension gratitude focuses on the person of the Lord – His love, integrity, glory, and power.

They praised him in their distress

Another example of a miracle arising out of third dimension gratitude is seen in the lives of Paul and Silas in Acts 16: 22-26:

> [22] *Then the multitude rose up together against them; and the magistrates tore off their clothes and commanded them to be beaten with rods.* [23] *And when they had laid many stripes on them, they threw them into prison, commanding the jailer to keep them securely.* [24] *Having received such a charge, he put them into the inner prison and fastened their feet in the stocks.* [25] *But at midnight Paul and Silas were praying and singing hymns to God, and the prisoners were listening to them.* [26] *Suddenly there was a great earthquake, so that the foundations of the prison were shaken; and immediately all the doors were opened, and everyone's chains were loosed.*

In this story, Paul and Silas were in dire straits. Not only had they been whipped and thrown into prison; but they were also bound in stocks and locked in the deepest parts of a dark dungeon. They were also badly wounded. There they were languishing in a foreign jail with no friends to bail them out. There was no way out of their hopeless situation.

Given their awful circumstances, it did not make sense to show gratitude. Nothing in their dire situation could be identified as a reason for gratitude. Yet they showed gratitude anyway. They praised God from the discomfort of their stocks.

Their radical act of third dimension gratitude released the Lord to perform a miracle that had not previously been reported in scripture: The Lord created a controlled earthquake that did not kill a single person. Instead, it conveniently unlocked all the doors and miraculously broke everyone's chains. And somehow, nobody was hurt. What an incredible miracle. But by expressing third dimension gratitude, Paul and Silas gave the Lord permission to wow them (and us).

Third dimension gratitude is about relationship

Third dimension gratitude only makes sense in the context of relationship. Paul and Silas praised the Lord in spite of their distress because they walked in relationship with Him. They recognized that although their circumstances had changed, the Lord was still the same. So, they trusted Him to work through their circumstances to bring about their ultimate good (Romans 8:28). Therefore, they were not distracted by the physical circumstances of their environment. Instead, they were focused on the unfailing faithfulness of the One in charge of their environment. Thus, they were able to express third dimension gratitude because their relationship with the Lord remained intact.

Third dimension gratitude only makes sense because it closes its eyes to what can be seen and looks to the One who is unseen. Third dimension gratitude says, "Lord, you matter more than all the things I see before me." Third dimension gratitude understands that the Lord is always good, no matter the circumstances. Therefore, third dimension gratitude praises the Lord, not for what He can do; but for who He is.

The relationship context of third dimension gratitude gives the Lord freedom of expression. Because relationship relies on mutual respect and give and take, third dimension gratitude cannot be used as a gimmick to "twist the Lord's arm" into doing something He does not want to do. Because it comes from a place of love, third dimension gratitude gives the Lord the freedom to act or not act. This important relationship principle is nicely expressed in the following scripture about Shadrach, Meshach, and Abednego:

> *16 Shadrach, Meshach, and Abed-Nego answered and said to the king, "O Nebuchadnezzar, we have no need to answer you in this matter. 17 If that is the case, our God whom we serve is able to deliver us from the burning fiery furnace, and He will deliver us from your hand, O king. 18 But if not, let it be known to you, O king, that we do not serve*

THE MIRACLE OF GRATITUDE

your gods, nor will we worship the gold image which you have set up."
(Daniel 3: 16-18)

Shadrach, Meshach, and Abednego did not prescribe a solution for the Lord. They declared, "we are sure our God will save us; but even if He doesn't . . ." This declaration showed their complete trust in the Lord and recognition of His sovereign right to choose. They did not control the outcome; the Lord did. And, because they regarded the Lord as an individual who makes His own decisions, they did not presume to tell Him how to glorify Himself. They were prepared to accept death as a possible outcome that could bring the Lord glory. Because only the Lord could define what brings Him glory, they would accept whatever outcome the Lord chose. They trusted the Lord, and the fiery furnace that burned before them would not take away their trust in Him.

From Shadrach, Meshach, and Abednego's story, we see that third dimension gratitude does not presume to tell the Lord what to do. Rather, third dimension gratitude gives the Lord creative freedom.

For this reason, third dimension gratitude is primarily expressed by believers who trust in the Lord. True believers don't say, "I will believe the Lord only after He saves me." They say, "Lord, whether you save me or not, I believe You." They express the same unshakeable belief in the Lord as Job who said:

Though He slay me, yet will I trust Him. (Job 13:15a)

THIRD DIMENSION GRATITUDE

Therefore, third dimension gratitude is expressed by believers who do not put the Lord in a box or pre-specify a course of action that is acceptable to them. Third dimension gratitude is expressed by believers who see the Lord as an individual who has His own thoughts and plans that may be different from our own (Isaiah 55:8). Third dimension gratitude is expressed by believers who do not tell the Lord how He should glorify Himself; but who release the Lord to do what He pleases.

Third dimension gratitude practice

Now, you have a chance to practice some third dimension gratitude. Think about your current life circumstances. What are some things happening in your life right now that do not look good? What are some "sink or swim" situations before you today? What are some "realities" you need to ignore to focus on the Lord? Let's not wait for the deliverance to express our gratitude. Let's thank the Lord for who He is right now. Let's practice now.

First thank the Lord for who He is. Thank Him for His integrity, power, awesomeness, and love. Thank Him for His faithfulness and for all the good things He has in store for you. Now thank Him for what He plans to do, even though you don't know what it will be. Thank Him for what He has already done in your situation, even if you have not seen it yet. Thank Him for those things not yet done. Finally, thank Him again for who He is.

THE MIRACLE OF GRATITUDE

Well done! Third dimension gratitude is hard because it needs you to close your eyes to the real and challenging situation before you to acknowledge the Lord, who is invisible. As you practice third dimension gratitude, you will find that it becomes easier to do over time.

Now that you understand third dimension gratitude, you will need the key to unlock the secret that keeps you consistently walking in a third dimension gratitude relationship with the Lord. This secret sauce lies in the unseen fourth dimension.

The Unseen Fourth Dimension

For God so loved the world that He gave His only begotten Son, that whoever believes in Him should not perish but have everlasting life.

(John 3:16)

The Word found me

When I was a child, I struggled with the concept of God. How could someone so important be so invisible? What was He hiding? Why didn't He reveal Himself? Why didn't He show me signs so I could know beyond the shadow of a doubt that He was real? Was He real? I wasn't sure. But we were supposed to serve Him, said my parents. They felt that it was important that we go to church, so I went with them. I mostly didn't like being at church; but I loved my parents and worked hard to please them. So, whatever my parents did, I did. When Mom and Dad fasted, I fasted too. When they prayed, I did too. I figured that God, whoever He was, was very lucky to have a dutiful person like me.

A time came when I left home to go to boarding school. I was on my own, away from Mom and Dad. I lived in the strict and regimented environment of a Catholic-run boarding school and, as a rule-follower (most of the time), I thrived. I lived by the school bell, which told me what to do. The bell rang; I woke up from sleep. It rang again; I went to breakfast. Another ring and I went to classes. All day long, the bell rang to remind me what to do; and I did it. My bell-led routine continued until the day ended with evening prayer. Our prayer times, which included morning prayer, prayer before meals, and the daily Rosary, reminded us that God, though unseen, was very much a part of our daily routine. We prayed regularly to God, and the Reverend Sisters often talked about Him. Clearly He was important to our existence; but He was somewhat off in the background. So, I didn't think too much about Him until, suddenly, I did.

A day came when my Uncle Sunny returned from living in Israel, bringing for me the gift of a Jerusalem Bible. This Bible was not my first – we were required to own one for school – but it was different from any Bible I had previously owned or seen. Its cover was made of wood, and its pages had gold edge gilding. Inside were photographs of places in Israel that marked where Jesus had been. Inside panels contained excerpts about the historicity of scripture. I was intrigued. This Bible was a fascinating piece of both art and literature. So, I opened its pages and love was born.

I didn't read this Bible; I devoured it. I couldn't get enough of it. I started at Genesis, read all the way to Revelation, and then read it all over again. I read this Bible when I woke up in the morning and before I went to bed at night. In the afternoon, I ignored the siesta (nap time) bell and read it instead of sleeping. I just couldn't get enough of this incredible book. I loved it. I read it, and read it, and read it again. Once, it fell into a bucket of water and I recovered it. Its wood cover eventually fell off and its pages turned moldy; but still I read it. Its pages stuck together, and when I tried to pry them apart, they tore. And still I read it. I kept reading this moldy, smelly, torn Jerusalem Bible until it fell apart and it didn't make sense to read it anymore.

This experience marked the beginning of my love of the Word, which has continued ever since. Although I eventually (reluctantly) gave up my beloved Jerusalem Bible, I found other acceptable substitutes. Over time, I acquired two to four heavy Bibles in different translations that I would spread out on my bed and read simultaneously. Fortunately, the internet was created and now, I can read my "Bible" on my tablet or online. And now, as the Holy Spirit reminds me of things I have read in the past, I recognize that the Bible no longer exists just in tangible format. It exists on the pages of my heart.

I started with a Bible and discovered the Word. This Word was alive and intriguing, mysterious and beautiful. This Word would speak to me, interpret my thoughts, and lead me to peace. This Word was in my daytime thoughts and my nighttime dreams. And, slowly, imperceptibly, and steadily, this Word led me to discover and love the Lord. Through this Word, I came to discover the One whom I had never known but who had always known me. I met the One who had been invisible to me yet was always present. I came to know the One who would perform no sign for me but was always demonstrating His wonders in every day small miracles.

This Word brought me to the Lord. And since it came into my life, I have never been the same. This Word was, is, always has been, and always will be, Jesus.

Gratitude is an equal opportunity producer

In this book, my focus has been on gratitude expressed to the Lord; however, expressions of gratitude do not have to directly involve the Lord. Gratitude can be expressed to anyone and anything. I show gratitude to my mom and dad for their sacrifice. I show gratitude to my computer for its faithful service. I show gratitude to my car for running smoothly. I show gratitude for the trees that rustle softly and birds that chirp sweetly. There is nothing to and for which I cannot express my gratitude.

Also, as we see in second dimension gratitude, the benefits of gratitude accrue to anyone who expresses it, whether it is to the Lord, people, or inanimate objects. The benefits of gratitude accrue to everyone, regardless of their faith, spiritual, or agnostic beliefs. Gratitude is a principle that works for everyone who practices it, no matter who they are.

See, the expression of gratitude is an acknowledgement that something good has occurred. Gratitude is a sign of recognition and appreciation that a gift that has been given. Gratitude is a sign that a person has removed themselves as the center of attention and looked beyond themselves to discover what lies beyond. Thus, gratitude is a sign that the expresser of it is paying attention.

People who pay attention and show gratitude discover beauty, love, peace, hope, and faith, and joy. People who pay attention can look beyond disappointment and see possibility. These gifts of keen observation and deep insights are gifts bestowed by gratitude. Therefore, gratitude is the gift that helps you see what is good even when you are surrounded by what is not good. Thus, our ability to show gratitude is God-given.

Gratitude replicates what the Lord did in creation when He looked at everything He had made and declared it to be good (Genesis 1). Every day of creation, the Lord looked upon His handiwork and declared it to be "good." At creation's grand finale, He looked upon all creation and declared it to be "very good." Therefore, when we recognize things around us to be good by demonstrating our gratitude, we follow the Lord's pattern of recognizing the Lord's creation as good, which is what He created it to be.

For this reason, every expression of gratitude directed toward the Lord, or His creation, is an acknowledgement of Him. It is an expression of recognition of a space that exists outside yourself. People who are self-centered do not easily show gratitude. Because they consider themselves to be the source of all things, it can be difficult for them to utter the simple words, "Thank you," because it would force them to acknowledge an outside influence upon their lives. In contrast, people who express gratitude show grace. And by expressing gratitude, they acknowledge God as good, even though they may not yet acknowledge Him as Lord.

Therefore, all gratitude points to the Lord as the source of all goodness and the maker of all creation. For this reason, first dimension and second dimension gratitude can be expressed by anyone. People expressing first or second dimension gratitude are not required to be believers. They don't need to profess faith in God to walk in first and second dimension miracles. All people can receive the benefits of gratitude because these benefits are governed by a key spiritual principle – you reap what you sow (Galatians 6:7). Therefore, you will always get more of what you create. If you do not create a thing, you may or may not get it; but if you create it, then as the creator, you will always have it. So, first and second dimension gratitude apply to and can be practiced by all people. However, third dimension gratitude is for those who acknowledge the creator of all things.

Third dimension gratitude acknowledges the Creator

So, while people who practice first and second dimension gratitude can do so while oblivious to the Lord's existence, people who practice third dimension gratitude see beyond creation to acknowledge the Lord's role in creation. They recognize that the

Lord who created all things can still create, and is still creating, new things today.

We may erroneously believe that creation ended a long time ago in the book of Genesis. However, creation did not end (or begin) in Genesis. From the moment the Lord created Adam and Eve, He turned over the primary work of creation to people (Genesis 1:28). For this reason, creation continues today.

Creation is an ongoing partnership between the Lord and people. This evolving creation story is seen in the volcanic eruption that creates a new land mass;[8] the unborn baby in the womb that is actively growing new organs and bones;[9] and in the new technologies being invented daily, each new version eclipsing the last. Therefore, the work of creation never stops but is always ongoing.

People who live in third dimension gratitude recognize this principle of ongoing creation. They see that new and miraculous things are constantly being created and know that the creation process can be accelerated by the hand of the Lord (1 Kings 18:46).

---

[8] 'Volcanic Eruption Creates a New Island in the South Pacific | Smart News | Smithsonian Magazine' <https://www.smithsonianmag.com/smart-news/volcanic-eruption-creates-a-new-island-in-the-south-pacific-180980838/> [accessed 14 April 2023].
[9] American Pregnancy Association, 'Baby Development Month By Month', *American Pregnancy Association*, 2022 <https://americanpregnancy.org/healthy-pregnancy/week-by-week/baby-development-month-by-month/> [accessed 14 April 2023].

THE MIRACLE OF GRATITUDE

This creative license of the Lord's is acknowledged by people who practice third dimension gratitude. Third dimension gratitude acknowledges that the Lord can create new things at any time and releases Him to create new things as He sees fit. Therefore, true third dimension gratitude occurs in the space of relationship, which is not possible without the Lord Jesus.

The Lord Jesus is the Word

The Lord Jesus is the human manifestation of the Word of God, which was spoken at the beginning of creation. This revelation comes to us from John 1:1.

> *¹ In the beginning was the Word, and the Word was with God, and the Word was God. ² He was in the beginning with God. ³ All things were made through Him, and without Him nothing was made that was made. ⁴ In Him was life, and the life was the light of men. ⁵ And the light shines in the darkness, and the darkness did not comprehend it.*

This scripture tells us about the role of the Lord Jesus in creation. It also tells us that the Lord Jesus is the Word. This concept is explained to us in John 1:14-18:

> *¹⁴ And the Word became flesh and dwelt among us, and we beheld His glory, the glory as of the only begotten of the Father, full of grace and truth. ¹⁵ John bore witness of Him and cried out, saying, "This was He of whom I said, 'He who comes after me is preferred before me, for He was before me.' " ¹⁶ And of His fullness we have all*

received, and grace for grace. [17] For the law was given through Moses, but grace and truth came through Jesus Christ. [18] No one has seen God at any time. The only begotten Son, who is in the bosom of the Father, He has declared Him.

Jesus is the Word who existed with God from the beginning. He is the reason why all things exist. He is the creative force behind everything we see in the universe. He is the author of all creation. For this reason, to connect with the Word is to connect with God. This connection is made possible through the Lord Jesus.

When the Lord Jesus came to the earth, He came to save people from their sins (Matthew 1:21). He came at a time when the Jewish people were under political oppression from the Roman Empire. People were treated unjustly; unbearable taxes were levied; and people were killed indiscriminately. But in the midst of the bad political climate, His singular focus was sin.

The Lord Jesus's extreme focus on sin appears baffling in light of the political problems going on in His day. The people needed deliverance from their political oppressors. In fact, they saw the Lord Jesus as a strong candidate for leadership (John 6:15). However, He stayed stubborn in His singular pursuit of sin.

The Lord Jesus understood sin to be the source of all the problems facing the world. He understood sin to be the real reason there was political turmoil. But most importantly, He understood sin to be the key obstacle separating us from true relationship with the Lord

THE MIRACLE OF GRATITUDE

God (Isaiah 59:2). For this reason, His primary mission was to deliver us from the bondage of sin.

The Lord Jesus lived a perfectly sinless life so that He could be the perfect sinless sacrifice (Leviticus 16:15-22). He died on the cross so that the punishment for our sin – past, present, and future – would come upon Him (Romans 3:25).

And because the Lord Jesus took away our sin, through Him, we have right standing with the Lord God, our Father. Every time we approach the Father through the lens of the sacrifice of the Lord Jesus, the Father no longer sees our sin because all our sins are taken away in Jesus. Instead, the Father sees us through the sacrifice of Jesus. He sees that we are spotless and without blemish. Only then is He able to walk in relationship with us.

And why would the Father want to walk in relationship with us? Because He loves us. He formed us for Himself. Therefore, it grieves Him when He cannot be in relationship with us. For this reason, He allowed Jesus to come to the earth and be born as a child so that He would pay the ultimate price, which we could not afford. He let Jesus walk through the pain of crucifixion so that we could be reconciled to Him.

He wants you. He wants to be in relationship with you. He wants to walk with you, talk with you, and share His goodness with you. It is for this reason that people who walk in any dimension of gratitude experience more of His goodness than others around them. It is also for this reason that people who walk in third dimension gratitude experience more of His unusual supernatural goodness. He wants to shower us all in His love because He delights in affirming our trust in Him.

But how do you walk in relationship with a God who is invisible? This question is the same one at which I stumbled as a child. Why is He invisible? What if I told you that He is not invisible? What if I showed you that how you see Him is a function how what part of your vision you use to see Him. See, God is Spirit. And those who worship Him, walk with Him, and talk with Him must engage with Him through the Spirit. The Lord Jesus gives us this information in John 4:23-24.

> ^{23} *But the hour is coming, and now is, when the true worshipers will worship the Father in spirit and truth; for the Father is seeking such to worship Him. ^{24} God is Spirit, and those who worship Him must worship in spirit and truth.*"

If we would enter into relationship with the Lord, we need to do it in Spirit and in truth. To engage the Lord as Spirit, we enter into the quiet place of spirit.

Engaging with the Spirit is very difficult for us because our orientation is strongly toward the things that we can see, hear, touch, and feel. We easily discard our thoughts and feelings because they don't seem tangible enough. Yet, the things we discard as intangible – thoughts and feelings – are the things that govern our lives, even when they are in the background where we don't obviously notice them. To engage with the Lord, we submit our thoughts and feelings to Him so that He can clear up the lines of communication and we can hear Him clearly – Spirit to spirit.

Wouldn't it be easier if the Lord would do something big and flashy, to show you that He really exists? Just once! Sometimes I wish He would; but the Lord is not big on doing signs to impress people. He does perform signs and wonders. He has been performing signs and wonders through the ages and is still performing them today. But most of His work throughout history has happened quietly and imperceptibly such that people who are not looking for Him may not find Him. Most of His great works have occurred seemingly by natural occurrences, in ways that people, in their logical minds, do not easily attribute them to Him. So, the tendency of people throughout history has been to make the error of attributing His greatness to themselves or to humans associated with His work.

Yet, our Lord has been at work all along, moving through the people we consider great. Throughout history, He has been sharing His ideas with them, opening doors of opportunity to them, and giving them a helping hand whenever they have been stalled in His work. Some of these "great people" have worked in active partnership with Him; but others have not. Yet, whether they or we acknowledge Him or not, our Lord, our Spirit God, is the force behind every move of history the world has ever known or will ever know (Amos 3:5). And when we sit in humility, removing the mocking and skeptical "logical" voice that clouds our judgement, we find that we can hear Him more clearly and it is then that we recognize that He has been speaking to us all along.

From the time that I was a little girl, the Lord had been calling to me. I asked questions about Him because He piqued my interest. I followed my parents in their religious practices because I wanted to know more about Him. I found Him on the pages of my Bible because I had quietly sought Him in my heart all this time.

But the true story of my finding Him is that He actually found me. He was the One who sowed questions in my mind that led me to a quiet and unthinking search for Him. He was the One who placed Himself on the pages of my Jerusalem Bible so I would find Him there. He is the One who, even now, plants questions in my heart so that He can answer them Himself. He is the one driving my quest for Him because He is the one who chose me. And He asked Jesus to pay an impossible price because I matter to him. And you matter to Him too.

You are the reason why the Lord Jesus paid the ultimate price with His life. He did it so that you too would have access to relationship with the Father. He led you through this book about gratitude so that you too would find Him on its pages. He gave me a message to preach about gratitude so that the opportunity could be created for you to answer His call.

THE MIRACLE OF GRATITUDE

I invite you to answer His call

How do you answer His call? You answer His call by saying "Yes." There are different ways to say that Yes. People who have gone before us have answered that call. Abraham said yes by leaving the land of his birth to travel to an unknown destination (Hebrews 11:8). Sarah said yes by receiving strength to conceive a child when it was biologically impossible (Hebrews 11:11). Noah said yes by accepting an assignment to build an ark where no natural disaster had ever occurred (Genesis 6). Esther said yes by accepting a mission that could have ended her life (Esther 4:16). Ruth said yes by abandoning her homeland to go with her mother-in-law to an unknown country (Ruth 1:16-17). Paul said yes by accepting a life as an outcast from his own people (Acts 28:27). Aquila and Priscilla said yes by teaching Apollos the scriptures (Acts 18:26). And I have said yes by writing you this book. As the Lord leads us on the unique path He has laid out for us, it is up to us to choose to say yes. How will you say yes today?

You can say yes by accepting the sacrifice of Jesus. You can say yes by accepting that you will never overcome sin without His help. You can say yes by laying down your life at His (Spirit) feet and taking up His Spirit life as your own. You can say yes by accepting the price that Jesus paid as a personal price that was especially for you. You can say yes by acknowledging that the price He paid enables you to walk in close communion with the Lord.

THE UNSEEN FOURTH DIMENSION

You say yes by answering the inner cry and hunger of your spirit. You say yes because it is the only logical answer to give when He calls you. You say yes because He deserves your yes. You say yes because He is your Father, and He wants you back.

I invite you to say yes today because your gratitude-filled miracle life only makes sense when it comes to be centered on the One who makes all gratitude possible.

The real miracle is you

If you were paying close attention in your reading of this book, you may have noticed something strange. Although I started with the title, "The Miracle of Gratitude," yet, over the course of this book, I have written about, not just one, but many miracles. While gratitude does indeed create many miracles, there is only one true miracle that counts. And that miracle, the most important one that gratitude creates, is you. Yes, the miracle of gratitude is you.

You are the real miracle of gratitude because of the transformation that gratitude brings to your life. As you show gratitude, moving from first, through second, to third dimension gratitude, you will find that there is a powerful transformation is happening inside you. As you embark on your journey of increasing in gratitude, you will find that you are no longer the person you used to be. Instead, is a newer, better, greater, and even more amazing version of you.

THE MIRACLE OF GRATITUDE

And it gets even better. As you enter in faith into the fourth dimension, receiving the Lord Jesus as your personal Savior, Lord, and Friend, your life becomes completely transformed until no one can recognize the you who first started this gratitude journey. You, my friend, are the final product of the effects of gratitude. The real miracle of gratitude is you.

And what a gift to the world you are and are becoming. What lives will be transformed through you. What abundance will be created in your environment through you because you chose today to partner with the Lord in transforming His world through creation. Thank you for everything you do and are as you walk in every dimension of gratitude. You are the miracle this world needs today. Thank you for stepping into the new, transformed, gratitude-filled you.

Conclusion

But the end of all things is at hand; therefore be serious and watchful in your prayers. (1 Peter 4:7)

We have come to the end of this book, and you stuck it out until the end. Well done! As I shared in the introduction, I am simply a sower who came to sow seed. I wrote this book not knowing that its seed would land with you. Now that you have received the seed of the Word, my work is done but yours is just beginning.

Now that the seeds have been sown, you get to decide what kind of ground you choose to be. Do you choose to be the ground that received seed by the wayside? "Wayside ground" is at risk of having the seed of the Word snatched away by the wicked one. Or do you choose to be the ground that received seed on stony places? "Stony ground" lacks depth and cannot endure life's challenges. Do you choose to be the ground that received the seed among the thorns? "Thorny ground" chokes up the time that would otherwise be spent discovering the Word. Or will you choose to be the good ground. "Good ground" is prepared to do the work that is needed to guarantee the harvest.

If you choose to be "good ground," then there is no time to lose. The work of tending the Word is only just beginning and will take your time and effort. You will need to find a water source and bring water to your fields to irrigate your ground. You will need to be vigilant about finding the right products that destroy pests without compromising the seed of the Word. You will need to watch vigilantly and be on your guard to do everything you can to support the coming harvest. And you will need to do all of it patiently because the harvest is coming. You don't yet know whether the harvest will produce 30-, 60-, or 100-fold. But the fold-increase is not your focus. Your focus is to tend the Word. And as long as you are consistently doing the work of tending the Word, your harvest is guaranteed.

As you practice the principles revealed to you in this book, the miracle of gratitude will operate in your life daily and become a source of blessing to you and others around you. I encourage you to become the good ground that prepares for the fruit of a great harvest that will bring the Lord great glory (John 15:8).

As you continually meditate on the words of this book, I pray that the Holy Spirit will multiply them to you and also use them to bless other people around you. You are the expression of God that people read. Therefore, may the gratitude you express in your life cause people to pause and begin to express gratitude and receive the real miracle of gratitude in their own lives as well.

Amen.

Acknowledgments

In keeping with the dimensions of gratitude, I would like to express my acknowledgments in the three dimensions.

First dimension gratitude

My first dimension gratitude starts with acknowledging the leadership of my pastor, Bisi Tofade, senior pastor of Jubilee Christian Church International Chapel of Victory in Durham North Carolina. It was Pastor Bisi who asked me to preach the message that became this book. When I asked Pastor Bisi, after the fact, why he selected me to preach the message, among so many other qualified people, he told me that he prayed about it, and the Lord told him. That explanation is characteristic of the kind of person that Pastor Bisi is – always seeking the Lord to know what the Lord would have him do. Therefore, I thank Pastor Bisi for listening to the Lord and asking me to preach the message. Without his asking me, this book would never have come to be – a true near miss gratitude experience if ever there was one.

Second dimension gratitude

In the spirit of second dimension gratitude, I want to thank all my pastors and leaders at Jubilee, represented here by both my senior pastors, Pastors Bisi and Toyin Tofade, who have pastored me for the last twenty years of my life at Jubilee. I thank God for the privilege to have as pastors men and women of God who have helped me grow in my walk with the Lord. My growth is a testament to God's grace upon your lives. Thank you.

I want specially to thank Pastor Toyin, who has led the charge for women at our church in which she has declared and shared messages from our church pulpit for over two decades. Pastor Toyin, your example is an inspiration and helps me to reach out for more than I ever thought possible.

I would like to thank my church family for the openness and kindness that they had to my preaching the message. If they were unwilling to receive the word of God through me, this book would also never have come to pass. Imagine if I had been booed off the platform. Where would this book be? For this reason, I thank my church family for their love and support, and for their willingness to follow the Lord's direction in allowing this unqualified woman to stand before them and share a message about gratitude.

I also want to my partners in ministry who helped with the audiovisual equipment on the day I preached the message. Special thanks to Cordell, Asa, Ellis, and Ayobami.

I want to thank my family, with whom I spent the week of Thanksgiving during which the message was conceived. Spending time with you on that farm in Adams, Tennessee, was an

ACKNOWLEDGEMENTS

incredible reminder to me of how good the Lord is and of His infinite wisdom and insight in bringing us together as a family.

I thank my mom and dad for the foresight they had in having four children. I thank them for encouraging us to believe in ourselves, and to reach for the heavens. Everything I do stems from my parents' message to me as a child that anything is possible, and that I can do all things. Thank you for gifting that to me.

I also want to thank Mom and Dad Onwuemene. Thank you for always supporting me, Chiedu, and the children. You are excited for the things that I accomplish and are proud of me. You love me unconditionally and I appreciate the joy that you bring to my life.

Next, I want to thank my siblings – the fires that forged me – Ife, Adeolu, and Tokunbo. It has been a privilege to do life with you over the last four decades. Thank you for sharpening me and for never being bashful about telling it like it is.

I also want to thank my bonus brothers and sisters – Gandhi, Awele, Renardo, Uchenna, and Oluchi. You accept me for who I am. I love that we get to share laughs and create new memories together. I appreciate you greatly.

I want to thank my children, Jonathan and Joelle, who bring such joy and delight to my life, daily. Your arrivals challenged me and caused me to return to my origins to question who I am and why I came. Everything I've ever accomplished is a testament to the

Lord's work through you. Your faiths encourage me and remind me of the true gift of trusting the Lord with childlike faith.

I also want to thank my nieces and nephews, Kayla, Natalie, Isaiah, Amarise, Jedidiah, Gabriel, Nathanael, and Evan. You all bring so much joy to my life. Every time I see you, I am reminded that the future is bright because it has you in it.

I want to thank my extended family, including my Uncle Sunny, Ngozi, Seun, Seyi, and Mary, Obong, Moyo, Grace, Mom and Dad Olagunju Oyin, Jide, Eni, Tolu, and every member of my extended family, who is not named here. Even though I don't list everyone by name, you are important to me. Know that I appreciate you all standing as one to encourage and support me. I appreciate you.

I want to say a special thank you to Uncle Sunny for gifting me the Jerusalem Bible that changed my life forever. Thank you for being an instrument of the Lord to transform my life permanently.

I also want to thank my work family for all they have done to help sharpen me. Your influence in my life helped me look inward to discover who I am and how I want to live my one earthly life. I am grateful for the environment in which I work and the flexibility it gives me to explore every facet of who I am in Christ.

I would like to specially thank Kate Epstein of Epsteinwords Editing Services for her attention to detail in providing copy edits.

ACKNOWLEDGEMENTS

Thanks also to Kayla Shuler, artist extraordinaire, for creating the cover art. Also, special thanks to my reviewers – Michael Onwuemene, Chiedu Onwuemene, and Pastor Bisi. This book would never have come together without your feedback. Thank you to the excellent staff at Amazon KDP, Apple Books, and other distributors for making copies available to readers all over the world.

Finally, I want to thank my husband and sweetie, Chiedu. Babe, since you came into my life, I have been able to reach for the stars and touch them. Thank you for everything you do to make this work possible. Thank you for every time you pick up the slack and do dishes or laundry or cook food because I am off doing some creative project. You are one in a million, Babe. What a privilege it is to walk this journey with you. I am grateful for you, who you are, what you do, And who you are becoming. Thank you also for pointing me to unveil the fourth dimension.

Third dimension gratitude

In the space of third dimension gratitude, I want to thank the Lord for everyone He will lead to read this book and for all the books that I will yet write. As of this writing, no one has yet read it. However, this book will be read by billions of people across many generations and will be translated into all languages of the world. Therefore, I also want to thank you, the reader, in advance for being courageous enough to pick up this book to read from it and learn from the principles expressed in it. I pray for you that you will walk more often in third dimension gratitude.

The unseen fourth dimension

And in the final, unseen fourth dimension, I want to thank the Lord Jesus, who came and made the biggest sacrifice ever. He laid down his life so that I could have access to a personal relationship with our Father. My joy and excitement in spending time with our Father and receiving revelation to write happened because the Lord Jesus made it possible. Therefore, Lord Jesus, I thank you for the sacrifice of Your life which makes my life possible. Thank you for bringing me up to be seated in position beside You. I also want to thank the person of the Holy Spirit who walks with me daily. I know that I am a son (daughter) of God because of Your leading in my life.

Finally, I want to thank the Lord and Father of our Lord Jesus Christ and my Father, the Lord God of heaven and earth, Creator of the universe. I want to thank You for choosing me when I didn't have any idea of who You are or why I needed You. Thank You for every door you open and for every door You close. Thank You for every opportunity You make available to me. I am nothing without You. Thank You for being the Lord of my life. What a privilege it is to walk with You daily. And Father, I will always walk with You because You will help me. As Your people read this book, may they be blessed and encouraged to walk with You.

ACKNOWLEDGEMENTS

Any other dimension I missed

To anyone I missed, know that I appreciate you and everything you do in my life to make the things I do a possibility. God bless you. And thank you for reading.

About the Author

Toyosi Onwuemene is a clinician researcher and entrepreneur whose early life ambition was to become a writer. Encouraged by family members to consider other careers that would pay the bills, she opted for a side job as a physician. Although she is now a hematologist, Toyosi's first love will always be writing. When she is not writing, Toyosi can be found creating something new in partnership with her Father, who still enjoys the thrill of creation. Toyosi is married to her sweetheart, Chiedu, with whom she has two incredible children.

Other Books by Toyosi Onwuemene

7 Laws of Black Hair

My Hair Is Beauty